OPEN BORDERS: THE IMPACT OF PRESIDENTIAL AMNESTY ON BORDER SECURITY

HEARING

BEFORE THE

COMMITTEE ON HOMELAND SECURITY
HOUSE OF REPRESENTATIVES

ONE HUNDRED THIRTEENTH CONGRESS

SECOND SESSION

DECEMBER 2, 2014

Serial No. 113–91

Printed for the use of the Committee on Homeland Security

Available via the World Wide Web: http://www.gpo.gov/fdsys/

U.S. GOVERNMENT PUBLISHING OFFICE

WASHINGTON : 2015

93–649 PDF

For sale by the Superintendent of Documents, U.S. Government Publishing Office
Internet: bookstore.gpo.gov Phone: toll free (866) 512–1800; DC area (202) 512–1800
Fax: (202) 512–2104 Mail: Stop IDCC, Washington, DC 20402–0001

COMMITTEE ON HOMELAND SECURITY

MICHAEL T. MCCAUL, Texas, *Chairman*

LAMAR SMITH, Texas
PETER T. KING, New York
MIKE ROGERS, Alabama
PAUL C. BROUN, Georgia
CANDICE S. MILLER, Michigan, *Vice Chair*
PATRICK MEEHAN, Pennsylvania
JEFF DUNCAN, South Carolina
TOM MARINO, Pennsylvania
JASON CHAFFETZ, Utah
STEVEN M. PALAZZO, Mississippi
LOU BARLETTA, Pennsylvania
RICHARD HUDSON, North Carolina
STEVE DAINES, Montana
SUSAN W. BROOKS, Indiana
SCOTT PERRY, Pennsylvania
MARK SANFORD, South Carolina
CURTIS CLAWSON, Florida

BENNIE G. THOMPSON, Mississippi
LORETTA SANCHEZ, California
SHEILA JACKSON LEE, Texas
YVETTE D. CLARKE, New York
BRIAN HIGGINS, New York
CEDRIC L. RICHMOND, Louisiana
WILLIAM R. KEATING, Massachusetts
RON BARBER, Arizona
DONDALD M. PAYNE, JR., New Jersey
BETO O'ROURKE, Texas
FILEMON VELA, Texas
ERIC SWALWELL, California
VACANCY
VACANCY

BRENDAN P. SHIELDS, *Staff Director*
JOAN O'HARA, *Acting Chief Counsel*
MICHAEL S. TWINCHEK, *Chief Clerk*
I. LANIER AVANT, *Minority Staff Director*

(II)

CONTENTS

OPEN BORDERS: THE IMPACT OF PRESIDENTIAL AMNESTY ON BORDER SECURITY

Tuesday, December 2, 2014

U.S. HOUSE OF REPRESENTATIVES,
COMMITTEE ON HOMELAND SECURITY,
Washington, DC.

The committee met, pursuant to call, at 9:05 a.m., in Room 311, Cannon House Office Building, Hon. Michael T. McCaul [Chairman of the committee] presiding.

Present: Representatives McCaul, Smith, King, Rogers, Miller, Meehan, Duncan, Chaffetz, Palazzo, Barletta, Hudson, Brooks, Perry, Sanford, Clawson, Thompson, Sanchez, Jackson Lee, Higgins, Keating, Barber, Payne, O'Rourke, Vela, and Swalwell.

Chairman McCAUL. The Committee on Homeland Security will come to order.

The committee is meeting today to hear testimony from Secretary Jeh Johnson on the administration's recent Executive Actions to grant temporary relief to millions of unlawful immigrants and the effect such actions will have on the security of our Nation's borders.

I now recognize myself for an opening statement.

Today we are here to talk about illegal immigration and the grave consequences of the administration's recent actions to bypass Congress. Immigration reform is an emotional and divisive issue; there is no doubt about that. But the President's unilateral actions to bypass Congress undermine the Constitution and threaten our democracy.

Let me be clear: Our immigration system is broken, and we need to fix it. America has always stood proudly as a beacon for hope for millions who are seeking a better life, and we should work hard to keep it that way. But regardless of where you stand on this issue, there is a right way to do this and there is a wrong way, and, unfortunately, the President has taken the wrong way.

In addition, the President has risked breaking something much more fundamental, and that is our democratic process. We are a Nation of laws. Yet this unprecedented Executive power grab undermines the principle that the people, not just one man, should be the ultimate decisionmakers in our country's most important political matters.

This action also has poisoned the well here in Washington at a time when Americans desperately want their Government to work together. We are facing crucial challenges that require Congress and the White House to cooperate, from combating overseas threats to driving economic growth. By making an end-run around Congress, the President has deliberately and willfully broken the trust that is needed between our branches of Government.

The President knows the damage of these actions. In fact, he has said over 20 times in his Presidency that he did not have the authority to take Executive Action on immigration and that this is, "not how democracy works."

He also said doing so will lead to a surge in more illegal immigration. He was right, and it will. History has proven that amnesty perpetuates a cycle of illegal entry into this country. This was true in the 1980s, and it has proven true under this administration's abuse of prosecutorial discretion—a power to decide when to prosecute law breakers and when not to, a power which should be used narrowly and carefully. This administration has done the opposite. They have taken a sweeping approach to prosecutorial discretion that makes a mockery of the law.

The consequences are very real. This summer, the administration's refusal to enforce our immigration laws enticed at least 60,000 unaccompanied children to make the perilous journey to our borders. Many traveled to the United States under misinformation regarding the administration's granting of permisos. We can expect many, many more to do the same because of the President's recent actions.

The lax interior enforcement policies adopted by this administration coupled with even the perception of amnesty become a powerful magnet that encourages more illegal immigration. We essentially tell citizens of other countries: "If you come here, you can stay. Don't worry, we don't deport you."

The reality on the ground is that, unless you commit multiple crimes, the chances of your being removed from this country are close to zero. This year, the U.S. Border Patrol apprehended almost 500,000 individuals along our Southern Border, but less than half were deported. Those who remained were given notices to appear before an immigration judge, with a court date years away, and released into the country. We know that the majority will never check back in with the authorities.

If we don't think that message is making its way back to Mexico and Central America, we are simply fooling ourselves. We will see a wave of illegal immigration because of the President's actions.

At its core, the President's unilateral amnesty plan is deeply unfair to the millions who are waiting in line to become a part of our great Nation, and it demonstrates reckless disregard for America's security. We have a formal immigration process for a reason: To promote fairness in allowing people to enter the United States and to keep those who will seek to do us harm outside of our borders.

Sadly, the Department of Homeland Security is unprepared to handle the coming surge that the President's policies will incite. The Border Patrol's resources are already strained as immigrants pour across the border, making it difficult to identify smugglers, criminals, and potential terrorists.

We need to reform our immigration laws, but we need to do it the right way, and that means starting the process in the lawmaking branch of our Government. Congress will address immigration reform, but we need to do so in an intelligent way and in keeping with the wishes of the American people. The majority of Americans do not agree with the President's Executive Actions. They want Congress to find a solution, one that begins with securing our borders.

I look forward to hearing from the Secretary, and I hope that he will address the serious concerns Congress and the American people have about the President's decision. We cannot turn a blind eye to the real threats which these actions will bring to our country's doorstep.

[The statement of Chairman McCaul follows:]

STATEMENT OF CHAIRMAN MICHAEL T. MCCAUL

DECEMBER 2, 2014

Today, we're here to talk about illegal immigration and the grave consequences of the administration's recent actions to bypass Congress. Immigration reform is an emotional and divisive issue; there is no doubt about that. But the President's unilateral actions to bypass Congress undermine the Constitution and threaten our democracy.

Let me be clear: Our immigration system is broken, and we need to fix it. America has always stood proudly as a beacon of hope for millions who are seeking a better life. And we should work hard to keep it that way.

But regardless of where you stand on this issue, there is a right way to do this, and there is a wrong way. And unfortunately the President has taken the wrong way.

In addition, the President has risked breaking something much more fundamental: Our democratic process. We are a Nation of laws. Yet this unprecedented Executive power grab undermines the principle that the people—not just one man—should be the ultimate decision makers on our country's most important political matters.

This action has also "poisoned the well" here in Washington at a time when Americans desperately want their Government to work together.

We are facing crucial challenges that require Congress and the White House to cooperate, from combating overseas threats to driving economic growth. But by making an end-run around Congress, the President has deliberately and willfully broken the trust that is needed between our branches of Government.

The President knows the damage of these actions. He has said over 20 times in his Presidency that he did not have the authority to take Executive Action on immigration, and that this is "not how democracy works." He also said doing so would, "lead to a surge in more illegal immigration." He was right. It will.

History has proven that amnesty perpetuates a cycle of illegal entry into this country. This was true in the 1980s and has proven true under this administration's abuse of "prosecutorial discretion"—a power to decide when to prosecute lawbreakers and when not to, a power which should be used narrowly and carefully. This administration has done the opposite. They've taken a sweeping approach to prosecutorial discretion that makes a mockery of the law.

The consequences are very real. This summer, the administration's refusal to enforce our immigration laws enticed at least 60,000 unaccompanied children to make the perilous journey to our borders.

Many travelled to the United States under misinformation regarding the administration granting of "permisos." We can expect many, many more to do the same because of the President's recent actions.

The lax interior enforcement policies adopted by this administration coupled with even the perception of amnesty become a powerful magnet that encourages more illegal immigration. We essentially tell citizens of other countries if you come here, you can stay—don't worry, we won't deport you. The reality on the ground is that unless you commit multiple crimes, the chances of your being removed from this country are close to zero.

This year the U.S. Border Patrol apprehended 479,000 individuals along the Southern Border but less than half were deported. Those who remained were given notices to appear before an immigration judge, with a court date years away, and released into the country. We know that the majority will never check back in with authorities.

If we don't think that message is making its way back to Mexico and Central America, we are simply fooling ourselves. We will see a wave of illegal immigration because of the President's actions.

At its core, the President's unilateral amnesty plan is deeply unfair to the millions who are waiting in line to become a part of our great Nation, and it demonstrates reckless disregard for America's security. We have a formal immigration process for a reason: To promote fairness in allowing people to enter the United States and to keep those who will seek to do us harm outside of our borders.

Sadly, the Department of Homeland Security is unprepared to handle the coming surge that the President's policies will incite. The Border Patrol's resources are already strained as immigrants pour across the border, making it difficult to identify smugglers, criminals, and potential terrorists.

We need to reform our immigration laws, but we need to do it the right way. And that means starting the process in the lawmaking branch of our Government. Congress will address immigration reform. But we need to do so in an intelligent way, and in keeping with the wishes of the American people. The majority of Americans do not agree with the President's Executive Actions. They want Congress to find a solution—one that begins with securing our borders.

I look forward to hearing from the Secretary, and I hope he will address the serious concerns Congress and the American people have about the President's decision.

We cannot turn a blind eye to the real threats which these actions will bring to our country's doorstep.

Chairman McCaul. With that, the Chairman now recognizes the Ranking Member.

Mr. Thompson. Thank you, Mr. Chairman, for holding today's hearing.

I would like to thank Secretary Johnson for making the time to be here to discuss recently announced Executive Actions on immigration and border security. As well as your fifth appearance before this committee in your short 12-month period shows that you are accessible, and I appreciate it.

Since 1956, Presidents have granted temporary immigration relief to impacted individuals on 39 separate occasions. Therefore, it would seem changes outlined by President Obama on November 20 are not outside the bounds of Presidential authority as provided under our Constitution.

Approximately 11 million undocumented individuals are forced to hide in the shadows, even as they live and work in plain sight in communities big and small across our Nation. Time and again, the House Republican leadership has been unwilling to act to fix our broken immigration system.

In the face of this crisis and the absence of Congressional action, the President acted in a measured way that is likely to improve both our Nation's security and economy. Specifically, the President announced an establishment of the Deferred Action for Parental Accountability program, which delays deportation for immigrants who have lived illegally in the United States for more than 5 years but have children who are citizens or have green cards.

Contrary to messaging from those who disagree with the President and many of his policies unrelated to immigration, this deferred action does not provide relief to recent border crossers. If the applicant can pass a criminal background check and pay a fee, he or she could qualify for a work permit and avoid deportation for 3 years at a time. Approximately 4 million immigrants are expected to qualify for this temporary relief.

This approach to provide deferred enforcement in order to keep families intact in light of Congressional failure to provide such relief is not novel. The Family Fairness Program, implemented by President Reagan and expanded by President George H.W. Bush, provided deferred enforcement for close family members of individuals legalized by the Immigration Reform and Control Act.

President Obama's directive rightly prioritizes the removal of undocumented individuals who have committed serious crimes, thus enhancing the safety of our communities.

I am troubled by the extreme criticism and disdain that this temporary and limited set of actions has received by some in Congress. The concept of families with working parents and children who attend school is consistent with the values we all hold. Now, with the President's announcement, this value or fabric of America is now being called ''renegade'' and a basis for more illegal action.

A fair criticism may be that vulnerable people in violence-ridden communities in Central America will be misled by enterprising coyotes and smugglers about the scope of individuals covered by the President's action. I look forward to hearing from Secretary Johnson about planning efforts that are being rolled out in anticipation of such misinformation.

We all know that recent border-crossers would not be covered. Even if there is an upsurge based on misinformation, Congress has made significant investment in personnel and equipment at the Southern Border that should ensure that DHS is able to effectively respond to any increases in attempted border crossings.

Let me be clear: The President's Executive Actions are a good start. However, there are still many people whom I believe deserve such consideration but are left out. Specifically, I would point to agricultural workers. The President's Executive Action does not provide specific relief to an estimated quarter-million of those workers that might be eligible for some type of deferred action. More remains to be done to address the labor needs for America's farmers. Where the Executive Action remains silent, there is an opportunity for Congress to legislate.

Let me close with two thoughts. To those who have said the President's actions do not represent the will of the American people, I say you need to listen better. Americans, by wide margins, believe our immigration system can be fixed in a fair and humane way that does not jeopardize our security.

Second, to those in Congress who have embraced the idea of putting the Department of Homeland Security in budgetary limbo while ever other Federal agency is funded for fiscal year 2015, I say you should really think about the message that sends about Congress' commitment to homeland security.

In closing, it is my hope that Congress will use this action as a starting point to legislate permanent fixes to our Nation's immigration system and further improve our border security. Mr. Chairman, I am willing to work with you throughout the remainder of this Congress and the next Congress to make these legislative changes happen.

I yield back.

[The statement of Mr. Thompson follows:]

STATEMENT OF RANKING MEMBER BENNIE G. THOMPSON

Since 1956, Presidents have granted temporary immigration relief to impacted individuals on 39 separate occasions; therefore, it would seem that changes outlined by President Obama on November 20 are not outside the bounds of Presidential authority, as provided under our Constitution.

Approximately 11 million undocumented individuals are forced to hide in the shadows even as they live and work in plain sight in communities big and small across our Nation. Time and again, the House Republican Leadership has been unwilling to act to fix our broken immigration system. In the face of this crisis and the absence of Congressional action, the President acted in a measured way that is likely to improve both our Nation's security and economy.

Specifically, the President announced an establishment of the Deferred Action for Parental Accountability Program—which delays deportation for immigrants who have lived illegally in the United States for more than 5 years but have children who are citizens or have green cards.

Contrary to messaging from those who disagree with the President and many of his policies unrelated to immigration, this deferred action does not provide relief to recent border crossers. If the applicant can pass a criminal background check and pay a fee, he or she could qualify for a work permit and avoid deportation for 3 years at a time.

Approximately 4 million immigrants are expected to qualify for this temporary relief. This approach—to provide deferred enforcement in order to keep families intact in light of Congressional failure to provide such relief—is not novel. The "Family Fairness" program implemented by President Reagan and expanded by President George H.W. Bush provided deferred enforcement for close family members of individuals legalized by the Immigration Reform and Control Act. President Obama's directive rightly prioritizes the removal of undocumented individuals who have committed serious crimes, thus enhancing the safety of our communities.

I am troubled by the extreme criticism and disdain that this temporary and limited set of actions has received by some in Congress. The concept of families with working parents and children who attend school is consistent with values we all hold. Now, with the President's announcement this value or fabric of America is now being called renegade and a basis for more illegal action.

A fair criticism may be that vulnerable people in violence-ridden communities in Central America will be misled by enterprising "coyotes" and smugglers about the scope of individuals covered by the President's actions. I look forward to hearing from Secretary Johnson about planning efforts that are being rolled out in anticipation of such misinformation. We all know that recent border crossers would not be covered.

Even if there is an upsurge based on such misinformation, Congress has made significant investments in personnel and equipment at the Southern Border that should ensure that DHS is able to effectively respond to any increases in attempted border crossings.

Let me be clear, the President's Executive Actions are a good start. However, there are still many people whom I believe deserve such consideration but are being left out. Specifically, I would point to agricultural workers.

The President's Executive Action does not provide specific relief to an estimated quarter million of these workers that might be eligible for some type of deferred action. More remains to be done to address the labor needs of America's farmers. Where the Executive Action remains silent, there is an opportunity for Congress to legislate.

Let me close with two thoughts. To those who have said that the President's actions do not represent the will of the American people, I say, you need to listen better. Americans, by wide margins, believe our immigration system can be fixed in a fair and humane way that does not jeopardize our security.

Second, to those in Congress who have embraced the idea of putting the Department of Homeland Security in budgetary limbo while every other Federal agency is funded for fiscal year 2015, I say "you should really think about the message that sends about Congress' commitment to homeland security."

In closing, it is my hope that Congress will use this action as a starting point to legislate permanent fixes to our Nation's immigration system and further improve our border security. Mr. Chairman, I am willing to work with you throughout the remainder of this Congress and next Congress to make these legislative changes happen.

Chairman McCAUL. I thank the Ranking Member. Other Members are reminded that statements may be submitted for the record.

[The statement of Hon. Jackson Lee follows:]

STATEMENT OF HONORABLE SHEILA JACKSON LEE

DECEMBER 2, 2014

Good morning and welcome. I would like to begin by thanking Chairman McCaul and Ranking Member Thompson for agreeing to convene this full committee hearing entitled, "Open Borders: The Impact of Presidential Amnesty on Border Security."

This is a very important matter, and as Ranking Member of the Homeland Security Border and Maritime Security Subcommittee, as well the Representative of the 18th Congressional District of Texas centered in Houston and located 300 miles from the Southwest Border. I appreciate your leadership in addressing the Department of Homeland Security's (DHS) efforts to secure our Nation's borders. Enhancing public safety along the Southwest Border remains an enormous priority for my Congressional district and the State of Texas.

I would like to also welcome our distinguished witness: Jeh Johnson, Secretary of the Department of Homeland Security.

The President has taken steps pursuant to his legal authority to fix our Nation's broken immigration system. The Executive Action prioritizes the deporting of felons, not families, and requires certain undocumented immigrants to pass a criminal background check and pay their fair share of taxes as they register to temporarily stay in the United States without fear of deportation.

The President's actions will streamline legal immigration to boost our economy and will promote naturalization for those who qualify.

The Executive Actions taken by the President will strengthen border security by adding 20,000 more Border Patrol Agents; crack down on companies who hire undocumented workers; create an earned path to citizenship for undocumented immigrants who pay a fine and taxes, pass a background check, learn English and go to the back of the line; and boost our economy and keeps families together by cutting red tape to simplify our legal immigration process.

The estimated number of undocumented immigrants in this country grew to a high of about 12.2 million in 2006, dropped to around 11.3 million, and has stopped growing for the first time since the 1980s.

The number of apprehensions, along our Nation's Southern Border has declined significantly; with the number now less than a third of what it was 12 years ago and today has reached the lowest level since the 1970s.

Immigration reform is good for the Nation and the economy. The benefit of immigration to the United States is evident in our National history. Immigrants represent the majority of our Nation's PhDs in math, computer science, and engineering, and over one-quarter of all U.S.-based Nobel laureates over the past 50 years were foreign-born.

Immigrants are also more than twice as likely as native-born Americans to start a business in the United States. They have started 1 of every 4 American small businesses and high-tech start-ups, and more than 40 percent of Fortune 500 companies were founded by immigrants or their children.

The President is asking Congress for a common-sense comprehensive immigration reform bill. This committee has already done this in a collegial bipartisan way when we drafted H.R. 1417, Border Security Results Act, which was passed by the Full Homeland Security Committee in May of 2013, and placed on the House Calendar where it has yet to be taken up for full House consideration. This bill would go a long way in addressing concerns regarding border security.

The President is offering a common-sense beginning, but only Congress can complete the work of comprehensive immigration reform.

This Executive Action is not a grant of amnesty for those who have entered the country unlawfully. It is an opportunity for the United States to create a stable environment for undocumented persons to come out of the shadows.

By the authority vested in the office of the President of the United States by the Constitution and the laws of this great Nation President Obama issued an order to modernize and streamline the U.S. immigration system, by directing that the following occur:

- Four million undocumented immigrants with no criminal record and who have lived in the United States for at least 5 years may now apply for a program that allows them to work and protects them from deportation, but does not create a path for legal residency or citizenship;
- An additional 1 million people may seek protection from immediate deportation;
- Through expansion of the existing program for "Dreamers," which President Obama announced previously will no longer be limited by age;
- No changes to the status of farm workers;

- None of the 5 million immigrants who are expected to have their status in the United States altered will receive any legal protections such as Government subsidies for health care under the Affordable Care Act; and
- Children who are American citizens but whose parents are undocumented will have access to Health Insurance, Medicaid, food stamps etc. These benefits will not extend to their non-citizen parents.

President Obama's actions do not create a path to citizenship nor do they give legal status to undocumented persons, only Congress can do that. President Obama's action on immigration is not new.

President Obama's actions fall within the scope of his Constitutional authority to prioritize Federal resources to focus on real threats to our Nation. Executive authority has been used by Presidents Dwight D. Eisenhower, Ronald Reagan, and George W. Bush to address deficiencies in how the Nation can best address the complex issue of immigration when Congress was unwilling or unable to provide a legislative solution.

Past Presidents have used their prosecutorial discretion authority to address immigration problems. President Obama has decided to use his Presidential prosecutorial discretion to prioritize Federal resources as they relate to removal of undocumented persons. Congress only provides enough funding to the Department of Homeland Security for about 400,000 deportations of undocumented persons each year.

President Obama's action does not create a path to citizenship nor does it prohibit Congress from acting or prevent the next President to issue another order to change the prosecutorial discretion outlined by this Executive Order.

Over a year ago, the Senate passed S. 744, Border Security, Economic Opportunity, and Immigration Modernization Act and referred it to the House for Consideration.

Today's hearing will allow Members of the committee to receive information on what the Department of Homeland Security has done to protect our Nation's borders and address the limited resources available for identifying undocumented persons for removal.

I look forward to Secretary Johnson's testimony. Thank you Mr. Chairman and I yield back the balance of my time.

Chairman McCAUL. We are pleased here today to have Secretary Jeh Johnson back to the committee. As always, we may not agree on all the issues, but we do so with civility.

Mr. Johnson, as many of you know, has a distinguished record, both at the Department of Defense and at the Department of Justice, and we appreciate your service with the Department of Homeland Security.

With that, you are recognized for an opening statement.

STATEMENT OF HONORABLE JEH JOHNSON, SECRETARY, U.S. DEPARTMENT OF HOMELAND SECURITY

Secretary JOHNSON. Thank you, Chairman McCaul, Ranking Member Thompson, committee Members here.

Let me begin by saying, in the same vein as the Chairman's remarks, we won't always agree, we have not always agreed, but I do appreciate the friendship and the collegiality that we enjoy between individual Members of this committee and their staffs and me and my staff.

This is the 12th time I have testified before Congress in 11 months, the fifth time before this committee. I feel like I know a number of you well.

On November 20, the President announced a series of Executive Actions to begin to fix our immigration system. The President views these actions as a first step toward reform of the system and continues to count on Congress for the more comprehensive reform that only legislative changes can provide.

The actions we took will begin to fix the system in a number of respects.

To promote border security for the future and to send a strong message that our borders are not open to illegal migration, we prioritize the removal of those apprehended at the border and those who came here illegally after January 1, 2014, regardless of where they are apprehended.

We also announced the next steps to strengthen our border security efforts as part of our Southern Border Campaign Strategy, which I first announced earlier this year.

To promote public safety, we made clear that those convicted of crimes, criminal street gang members, and National security threats are also priorities for removal.

To promote accountability, we encourage those undocumented immigrants who have been here for at least 5 years, have sons or daughters who are citizens or lawful permanent residents, and do not fall into one of our enforcement priorities to come out of the shadows, get on the books, and pass National security and criminal background checks. After clearing all their background checks, these individuals are eligible for work authorization and will be able to pay taxes and contribute more fully to our economy.

The reality is that, given our limited resources, these people are not—and have not been for years—priorities for removal. It is time we acknowledge that and encourage them to be held accountable. This is simple common sense.

To rebuild trust with State and local law enforcement which are no longer honoring ICE detainers, we are ending the controversial Secure Communities Program as we know it and making a fresh start with a new program that fixes existing problems.

To promote U.S. citizenship, we will enable applicants to pay the $680 naturalization fee by credit card and expand citizenship public awareness.

To promote the U.S. economy, we will take administrative actions to better enable U.S. businesses to hire and retain qualified, highly-skilled foreign-born workers.

The reality is that for decades Presidents have used Executive authority to enhance immigration policy. President Obama views these actions as a first step toward the reform of the system and continues to count on Congress for the more comprehensive reform that only changes in law can provide. I would like to add to that: I, too, would welcome the opportunity to work with Members of this committee on comprehensive immigration reform legislation.

I recommended to the President each of the Homeland Security reforms to the immigration system that he has decided to pursue. These recommendations were the result of extended and candid consultations I had with the leadership of Immigration and Customs Enforcement, Customs and Border Protection, and U.S. Citizenship and Immigration Services. Along the way, I also spoke with members of the workforce who implement and enforce the law to hear their views. In my own view, any significant change in policy requires close consultation with those who administer the system.

We also consulted a wide range of stakeholders, including business and labor leaders, law enforcement officers, religious leaders, and Members of Congress from both sides of the aisle. We also consulted with the Department of Justice, and we received a formal written opinion from the Justice Department's Office of Legal Counsel concerning enforcement prioritization and deferred action, and that opinion has been made public.

Thank you for your attention to these remarks. I look forward to your questions.

[The prepared statement of Secretary Johnson follows:]

PREPARED STATEMENT OF HON. JEH C. JOHNSON

DECEMBER 2, 2014

Thank you Chairman McCaul, Ranking Member Thompson, and committee Members for the opportunity to testify today.

On November 20 President Obama announced a series of Executive Actions to begin to fix our immigration system. The President views these actions as a first step toward reform of the system, and continues to count on Congress for the more comprehensive reform that only legislative changes can provide.

The actions we took will begin to fix the system in a number of respects.

To promote border security for the future, and to send a strong message that our borders are not open to illegal migration, we prioritize the removal of those apprehended at the border and those who came here illegally after January 1, 2014, regardless of where they are apprehended. We also announced the next steps to strengthen our border security efforts as a part of our Southern Border Campaign Strategy, which I first announced earlier this year.

To promote public safety, we make clear that those convicted of crimes, criminal street gang members, and National security threats are also priorities for removal.

To promote accountability, we encourage those undocumented immigrants who have been here for at least 5 years, have sons or daughters who are citizens or lawful permanent residents, and do not fall into one of our enforcement priorities, to come out of the shadows, get on the books, and pass National security and criminal background checks. After clearing all their background checks, these individuals are eligible for work authorization and will be able to pay taxes and contribute more fully to our economy. The reality is that, given our limited resources, these people are not priorities for removal—it's time we acknowledge that and encourage them to be held accountable. This is simple common sense.

To rebuild trust with State and local law enforcement which are no longer honoring ICE detainers, we are ending the controversial Secure Communities program as we know it, and making a fresh start with a new program that fixes existing problems.

To promote U.S. citizenship, we will enable applicants to pay the $680 naturalization fee by credit card and expand citizenship public awareness.

To promote the U.S. economy, we will take administrative actions to better enable U.S. businesses to hire and retain qualified, highly-skilled foreign-born workers.

The reality is that, for decades, Presidents have used Executive authority to enhance immigration policy. President Obama views these actions as a first step toward the reform of the system, and continues to count on Congress for the more comprehensive reform that only changes in law can provide.

I recommended to the President each of the Homeland Security reforms to the immigration system that he has decided to pursue. These recommendations were the result of extended and candid consultations I had with the leadership of Immigration and Customs Enforcement (ICE), Customs and Border Protection (CBP) and U.S. Citizenship and Immigration Services (USCIS). Along the way, I also spoke with members of the workforce who implement and enforce the law to hear their views. In my own view, any significant change in policy requires close consultation with those who administer the system. We also consulted a wide range of stakeholders, including business and labor leaders, law enforcement officers, religious leaders, and Members of Congress from both sides of the aisle. We also consulted with the Department of Justice, and we received a formal, written opinion from the Justice Department's Office of Legal Counsel concerning enforcement prioritization and deferred action, and that opinion has been made public.

Here is a summary of our Executive Actions:

Strengthening border security. Our Executive Actions emphasize that our border is not open to future illegal migration and that those who come here illegally will be sent back, unless they qualify for some form of humanitarian relief under our laws. The reality is that, over the last 15 years spanning the Clinton, Bush, and Obama administrations, much has been done to improve border security. But, through the Executive Actions announced last week, we can and will do more.

Today, we have unprecedented levels of border security resources—personnel, equipment, and technology—along our Southwest Border. This investment has produced significant positive results. Apprehensions have declined from over 1.6 million in 2000 to around 400,000 a year—the lowest rate since the 1970s. According to Pew Research, the number of undocumented immigrants in this country grew to a high of 12.2 million in 2007 and has remained, after a slight drop, at about 11.3 million ever since. That means this population has stopped growing for the first time since the 1980s, and over half of these individuals have been in the United States for 13 years.

Without a doubt, we had a setback this summer. We saw an unprecedented spike in illegal migration into South Texas—from Guatemala, Honduras, and El Salvador. And as everyone knows, it consisted of large numbers of unaccompanied children and adults with children. We responded with more security and law enforcement resources; more processing centers; more detention space; more Border Patrol Agents in the Rio Grande Valley; more prosecution of criminal smuggling organizations; an aggressive public message campaign; engagement of Central American leaders by the President and the Vice President; and increased interdiction efforts by the government of Mexico. And, since the spring, the numbers of unaccompanied children crossing the Southern Border illegally have gone down considerably: May–10,578; June–10,620; July–5,499; August–3,138; September–2,426; October–2,529.

However, we are not finished with the work of securing our border. We can and will do more—that's a critical component of the President's Executive Actions.

We will build upon the border security infrastructure we put in place last summer. We announced several days ago the opening of another detention facility for adults with children in Dilley, Texas, that has the capability to detain over 2,000 individuals. At the same time, we will close the smaller, temporary facility for adults with children at Artesia, New Mexico. We are developing a "Southern Border Campaign Strategy" to fundamentally alter the way in which we marshal resources to the border under the direction of three new Department task forces. They will follow a focused risk-based strategy, with the overarching goals of enforcing our immigration laws and interdicting individuals seeking to illegally cross land, sea, and air borders. These actions are designed to send a clear message: In the future, those who attempt to illegally cross our borders will be sent back.

Creating new and clearer enforcement prioritization policies.—This new policy will also have a strong border security component to it, in addition to prioritizing for removal public safety and National security threats. Virtually every law enforcement agency engages in prosecutorial discretion. With the finite resources an agency has to enforce the law, it must prioritize use of those resources. To this end, DHS will implement a new and clearer enforcement and removal policy. The new policy places: (i) Top priority on National security threats, convicted felons, criminal gang participants, and illegal entrants apprehended at the border; (ii) second-tier priority on those convicted of significant or multiple misdemeanors and those who entered or re-entered this country unlawfully after January 1, 2014—regardless of whether they are apprehended at the border—or significantly abused the visa or visa waiver programs; and (iii) the lowest priority are those who are non-criminals but who have failed to abide by a final order of removal issued on or after January 1, 2014.

Giving people the opportunity to be held accountable.—The reality is that, undocumented immigrants who have been in this country for years, raising American families and developing ties to the community. Many of these individuals have committed no crimes and are not enforcement priorities. It is time that we acknowledge this as a matter of official policy and encourage eligible individuals to come out of the shadows, submit to criminal and National security background checks, and be held accountable.

We will therefore offer, on a case-by-case basis, deferred action to individuals who: (i) Are not removal priorities under our new policy, (ii) have been in this country at least 5 years, (iii) have sons or daughters who are U.S. citizens or lawful permanent residents, and (iv) present no other factors that would make a grant of deferred action inappropriate. The reality is that our finite resources will not and should not be expanded to remove these people. We are also amending eligibility for the Deferred Action for Childhood Arrivals (DACA) program. At present, eligibility is limited to those who were under 31 years of age on June 15, 2012, entered the United States before June 15, 2007, and were under 16 years old when they entered. We will amend eligibility for DACA to cover all undocumented immigrants who entered the United States before the age of 16, not limited to those born after June 15, 1981.

We are also adjusting the cut-off date from June 15, 2007 to January 1, 2010 and expanding the period of work authorization from 2 years to 3 years.

President Obama's administration is not the first to undertake such actions. In fact, the concept of deferred action is an established, long-standing administrative mechanism dating back decades, and it is one of a number of similar mechanisms administrations have used to grant temporary immigration relief for humanitarian and other reasons. For example, Presidents Reagan and Bush authorized Executive Action to shield undocumented children and spouses who did not qualify for legalization under the Immigration Reform and Control Act of 1986. This "Family Fairness Program" used a form of relief known at the time as "indefinite voluntary departure," which is similar to the deferred action authority we use today.

Fixing Secure Communities.—We will end the Secure Communities program as we know it. The overarching goal of the program is a good one, but it has attracted widespread criticism in its implementation and has been embroiled in litigation. Accordingly, we will replace it with a new "Priority Enforcement Program" that closely and clearly reflects DHS's new top enforcement priorities. The program will continue to rely on fingerprint-based biometric data submitted during bookings by State and local law enforcement agencies but will, for the most part, limit the circumstances under which DHS will seek an individual in the custody of State and local law enforcement—specifically, only when an individual has been convicted of certain offenses listed in Priorities 1 and 2 of our new enforcement priorities outlined above.

Pay reform for ICE ERO officers.—We will conduct an expeditious review of personnel reforms for Immigration and Customs Enforcement (ICE) officers engaged in removal operations, to bring their job classifications and pay coverage in line with other law enforcement personnel, and pursue regulations and legislation to address these issues.

Extending the provisional waiver program to promote family unity.—The provisional waiver program we announced in January 2013 for undocumented spouses and children of U.S. citizens will be expanded—to include the spouses and children of lawful permanent residents, as well as the adult children of U.S. citizens and lawful permanent residents. At the same time, we will clarify the "extreme hardship" standard that must be met to obtain the provisional waiver.

Supporting military families.—We will work with the Department of Defense to address the availability of parole-in-place and deferred action, on a case-by-case basis, for the spouses, parents, and children of U.S. citizens or lawful permanent residents who seek to enlist in the U.S. Armed Forces.

Increasing access to U.S. citizenship.—We will undertake options to promote and increase access to naturalization and consider innovative ways to address barriers that may impede such access, including for those who lack resources to pay application fees. To enhance access to U.S. citizenship, we will: (i) Permit the use of credit cards as a payment option, and (ii) enhance public awareness around citizenship. USCIS will also include the feasibility of a partial fee waiver as part of its next biennial fee study.

Supporting U.S. business and high-skilled workers.—Finally, DHS will take a number of administrative actions to better enable U.S. businesses to hire and retain qualified, highly-skilled foreign-born workers. For example, because our immigration system suffers from extremely long waits for green cards, we will amend current regulations and make other administrative changes to provide needed flexibility to workers with approved employment-based green card petitions.

Overall, the Executive Actions the President announced last week will not only bolster our border security, they will increase family unity, increase access to U.S. citizenship, grow and strengthen the competitiveness of the U.S. economy, and create jobs, particularly in the high-skilled labor sectors.

Again, the President views these actions as a first step toward the reform of our immigration system and he continues to count on Congress for the more comprehensive reform that only legislative changes can provide. In the mean time, we will use our Executive authority to fix as much of our broken immigration system as possible.

I look forward to answering your questions.

Chairman MCCAUL. I thank the Secretary.

The Chairman recognizes himself for 5 minutes for questions.

I would have to echo again, in my opening statement, there is a right way to do this and a wrong way. Obviously, I disagree with the President's approach in this case. Presidents Reagan and Bush worked with the Congress. Congress passed legislation that the

Presidents were implementing—a very strong distinction from the case that we have today.

My question—I have several questions. One, first, is the President said over 20 times that he did not have the legal authority to do this, to take this Executive Action, and that this is not how a democracy works. Do you agree with that prior statement?

Secretary JOHNSON. Chairman, I know from 30 years as a lawyer that when someone paraphrases remarks from somebody I want to see the full Q&A, I want to see the full context to know exactly what the person said.

I have looked at various excerpts of remarks by the President concerning his legal authority to act, and I do not believe that what we have done is inconsistent with that. In fact, we spent a lot of time with lawyers, and we spent a lot of time with DOJ's Office of Legal Counsel. They wrote what is, in my judgment, a very thoughtful 30-page public opinion on the available legal authority to act to fix——

Chairman McCAUL. I have no doubt about your actions after the election on this issue, but I will say I will be happy to provide you with the written statements that I have personally read to your office. It is confusing, and it poses a bit of hypocrisy, I think, to the American people because then, after the election, he reversed his course. After the election, he says that now he does have the legal authority to move forward.

So who should we believe—the President before the election who said he didn't have legal authority to take this action or the President after the election who says that he does have the authority to take this Executive Action?

Secretary JOHNSON. Congressman, what I know is we spent months developing these reforms, and we spent a lot of time with lawyers—very close consultation with lawyers. There were some things that they told us they thought we did not have the legal authority to do, which is reflected in the OLC opinion, and there are things they told us very clearly that we did have the legal authority to do.

The analysis was very thoughtful, very time-consuming, and very extensive. I am satisfied, as a lawyer myself and the person who has to come here and defend these actions, that what we have done is well within our existing legal authority.

Chairman McCAUL. Note, I have no doubt with respect to your integrity, but I think the timing of these statements makes it look more political to me, that this is a political decision rather than a policy decision. I know you have run this through all the legal traps, but I think that what we are concerned about are these prior statements that he didn't have legal authority and now he does. So perhaps he wasn't following the correct legal advice at one juncture or the other.

Did he get the right political or legal advice before the elections or after? Because he has changed his tune on this, and I think that is what is so confusing to Members of Congress and the American people about the authenticity of this President's decision.

Secretary JOHNSON. Well, you refer to timing. I originally received an assignment to look at our authority to take Executive Action in the spring, and we began to develop reforms in the spring.

We were urged by many in Congress to wait, and so we waited until the summer. We got to the summer; we were urged then to wait till late summer, which we did.

Once we knew the Speaker was not going to be able to marshal the votes in the House of Representatives for reform, we decided we were going to act in late summer. Then we were urged to wait till after the mid-terms, which we have done.

So we have waited a considerable amount of time, more than——

Chairman MCCAUL. My time is limited. I know you have, but it has undermined our Constitutional principles and our democracy by bypassing Congress.

He also stated earlier that this could lead to a surge in more illegal immigration. Do you agree with that statement by the President?

Secretary JOHNSON. No. In fact, we prioritize recent illegal migrants. We prioritize those who came here illegally after January 1, 2014.

I intend to highlight that fact wherever I go. In fact, I am going to our new detention facility in Dilley, Texas, week after next to highlight the fact that we have expanded our detention capability and recent arrivals illegally are priorities for removal. I intend to go to the country of Mexico to work with them on their own interdiction efforts.

So, wherever I go, I intend to highlight the fact that these new reforms prioritize recent illegal entrants.

Chairman MCCAUL. Again, I just look at history. In 1986, the amnesty law was passed, and it led to a wave of illegal immigration. I look at DACA. I had 60,000 children, unaccompanied, crossing my border in Texas through the Rio Grande Valley sector.

As a result of DACA, you can't deny that the traffickers are going to message this, now this Executive Action, and exploit it. I have had high-level people in the State Department tell me this. They are worried about this being taken down to the Central American countries and exploited, and we are going to see a surge and a wave of illegal immigrations.

I am telling you, it is going to happen. This Department needs to be ready for that, to protect the Nation from it, because it is coming. In my judgment, there is no question about it.

The last question is on fraud. Twenty percent of DACA applications are denied as fraudulent. We saw that after 1986. The 1993 World Trade Center bomber, one of them, had fraudulent documentations exploiting the 1986 amnesty law.

What are you going to do to verify that these people are not fraudulently entering the country, including what could be security threats to the country?

Secretary JOHNSON. Congressman, that is something that I, too, am concerned about. Fraudulent applications have the potential to undermine the whole process. So, in the implementation, in the planning for the implementation, I want to be sure that we take a hard look at best practices to avoid fraudulent applications, fraudulent misuse of the program. That is a priority of mine.

Chairman MCCAUL. Well, we look forward to working with you on that.

With that, now the Chairman recognizes the Ranking Member for questions.

Mr. THOMPSON. Thank you, Mr. Chairman.

Mr. Secretary, there are striking similarities between President Obama's Executive Action and those similar actions taken by President Reagan and President George H.W. Bush on addressing this.

Your statement to this committee is that the Department of Justice has provided authority by which the President is acting. Are you comfortable with that? Or did you participate after the issuance of that authority in the development of a recommendation to the President?

Secretary JOHNSON. Yes, sir.

Let me add this. Whenever I assess a legal question, both as a lawyer for the Department of Defense and now as a Cabinet Secretary, and the viability of a legal issue, I welcome a thorough opinion like the one we have from OLC, but I also ask myself, could I defend that action before a committee of Congress if called upon to do so? I am fully comfortable that we have the legal authority to push forward these reforms in particular.

Specifically with regard to deferred action, that is an authority that Presidents have used for decades, as you have been pointed out, in various different forms. That is noted in the OLC opinion. So I am fully comfortable that deferred action is an inherent Executive branch authority that can and should be used from time to time, and we have done so here.

Mr. THOMPSON. Well, I would like to add to that, in those other actions, Congress had not moved forward, and that was why President Reagan and George H.W. Bush did pursue the Executive Order route, because of the inaction of Congress.

So, while there are differences of opinion, I don't think there is a question that we have not done our job as Members of Congress, and the problem gets worse. Those 11 million people who are here we have to address.

Another issue that I am concerned about, Mr. Secretary: The Department's Unity of Effort. How will the Southern Border campaign address the challenges around that?

Secretary JOHNSON. The Southern Border campaign strategy that we are developing is an initiative to bring to bear all of the Department's resources in a particular region of the country on border security. We are, in my judgment, too stovepiped in that approach. CBP ICE, CIS, FEMA, the Coast Guard, we are too stovepiped, and we need to bring a more comprehensive strategic approach to it.

So what we are doing is creating two regional task forces—Joint Task Force West, Joint Task Force East—to focus on maritime border security in the Southeast, to focus on border security in the Southwest. I expect to announce the new leaders of those task forces very soon, and we are developing a time line for getting this done.

I issued, as part of these various directives here, a directive devoted toward the Southern Border campaign strategy and set forth here what the goals and lines of effort are to be.

As you know, I think we have received a lot of bipartisan support for this effort, and I intend to move forward with it.

Mr. THOMPSON. A comment has been made about the number of undocumented children coming in recent years. Your Department requested supplemental funding to address the needs to work with that. Congress did not give you the money.

Can you continue to maintain the level of support to address that issue if Congress continues to refuse to give you the money necessary to do that job?

Secretary JOHNSON. It will be very difficult.

We have as part of our fiscal year 2015 budget request a request for an additional $750 million. Most of that will go to expanded detention capability and resources. We set that up in response to the spike in illegal migration last summer, and we want to maintain that and we want to add to it.

So I referred to the new detention facility in Dilley, Texas, a moment ago. That is a capacity for up to 2,400 spaces. We need to pay for that. But it is a vital aspect of our Southern Border security, in my view.

Frankly, I am disappointed that the Congress has not supported us in that vital border-security effort. I hope the Congress will act to fund that and to fund the expanded flights, the repatriation, that we have developed since last summer. We need to pay for these things. I know every Member of this committee wants to support and enhance border security, so I am urging that Congress act on my request so we can pay for it.

Mr. THOMPSON. I yield back, Mr. Chairman.

Chairman MCCAUL. The Chairman recognizes the gentleman from Texas, Mr. Smith.

Mr. SMITH. Thank you, Mr. Chairman.

Mr. Secretary, what do you project to be the number of people coming across the border illegally this year?

Secretary JOHNSON. The number of people crossing the border illegally each year?

Mr. SMITH. Yes. Total number this year, what do you project?

Secretary JOHNSON. Fiscal year 2014, I believe that total apprehensions, which are an indication of total attempts to cross the border illegally, is about 479,000, 477,000.

Mr. SMITH. How many people will succeed in actually entering without being apprehended, would you guess?

Secretary JOHNSON. There is a calculation that is something in excess of that number. You add, as I am sure you know, apprehensions plus turn-backs plus what we call got-aways, and you get an estimate for total illegal migration.

Mr. SMITH. Right.

Secretary JOHNSON. I believe—but I would be happy to provide this number to you, what our Border Patrol's best estimate is—but I believe it is some percentage in excess of the 477,000, 479,000.

Mr. SMITH. Right. That is what I have heard. Over half a million people will succeed in coming into the United States illegally this year.

If you were to succeed in achieving your goal of operational control of the border, what would you like to get that number down to? From half a million to what?

Secretary JOHNSON. Well, very clearly, sir, I would like to see that number come down. In fiscal year 2000, we had 1.6 million apprehensions——

Mr. SMITH. Right. If I may interrupt you for a minute, what are your metrics in determining whether the border is secure or not?

Secretary JOHNSON. Well, the Border Patrol has metrics, and I have asked that they improve upon that. I recently issued a directive——

Mr. SMITH. Right.

Secretary JOHNSON [continuing]. To better define our border metrics and how we should define——

Mr. SMITH. Are there any metrics——

Secretary JOHNSON [continuing]. Border security. So that is a work in progress, sir.

Mr. SMITH. So you don't have the metrics today to determine whether the border is secure?

Secretary JOHNSON. The Border Patrol does have metrics, which I believe I have shared with various Members of this committee. I have asked that they refine that, and they are in the process of doing that.

Mr. SMITH. Okay. So, again, I don't think that we have the metrics we need to determine whether the border is security or not.

Let me read a sentence from page 3 of your statement today. "Our Executive Actions emphasize that our border is not open to future illegal immigration and that those who come here illegally will be sent back unless they qualify for some form of humanitarian relief under our laws."

Is it true, though, that the Department of Homeland Security is already releasing illegal immigrants from ICE custody or not?

Secretary JOHNSON. I am sorry. What was the last part of that question?

Mr. SMITH. Is the Department releasing illegal immigrants now from ICE custody instead of sending them home?

Secretary JOHNSON. I believe that we have a number of those who are released on bond, if I understand your question. Through a directive, I recently asked ICE to have a higher-level approval authority for when that happens.

Mr. SMITH. But, again, to put that in simple language, ICE is releasing individuals who are in the country illegally, which is contrary to your statement that they would be sent home.

It also seems to me contradicting your statement is the fact that very few individuals who have entered the country illegally who have not, in your terms, committed other serious crimes are going to be sent home. It is going to be a very, very small fraction; it may be 1 or 2 percent.

So I don't think your statement here is true, to say that those who come here illegally will be sent back. It is actually a very small subset of those who come into the country illegally.

Secretary JOHNSON. Well, let me say two things, sir.

During the summer, we dramatically reduced the repatriation time for adults from 33 down to 4 days.

Mr. SMITH. Yeah.

Secretary JOHNSON. We have built added detention space for family units, which I am hoping this Congress will support.

Mr. SMITH. That is nice, but that is not answering my question. Once again, you are not going to be sending people back home just because they are in the country illegally. In fact, I think you have just admitted ICE is already releasing individuals who could be returned home but are not being returned home.

Furthermore, I think you are also releasing individuals who have been convicted of crimes in the United States and putting them back out on our streets and in our communities.

Do you want to estimate how many thousands of people are being released who are criminal aliens? In the last several years, I think it totaled 30,000 people. Do you have any idea what it might be this year?

Secretary JOHNSON. The issue of release of those convicted of crimes is one that I have focused on for the last several months. So what I have directed to ICE is that there be a higher-level approval authority for a circumstance when somebody with a criminal record is released from immigration detention on bond.

I have also directed that a release of somebody with a criminal record should not occur because of fiscal constraints, and we will find a way to pay for that.

Mr. SMITH. I hope you can improve the situation because, as I say, right now you are releasing criminal aliens and you are releasing individuals who should be sent home. I don't think that is the way our laws should be enforced.

Thank you, Mr. Chairman. Yield back.

Chairman McCAUL. The Chairman now recognizes the gentlelady from Texas, Ms. Jackson Lee.

Ms. JACKSON LEE. Mr. Chairman and to the Ranking Member, again, let me thank you for this hearing. This is the important work of the United States Congress, is unbiased fact-finding.

Secretary, again, thank you for your service and the importance of your related service in the Department of Defense and, as well, your knowledge and work with the U.S. Department of Justice.

I, frankly, believe that we can clarify the President's comments, and he was, in fact, extremely consistent. I have a series of questions.

As I understand the Executive Order, it does not confer immigration status, nor does it confer a pathway to citizenship. Is that correct?

Secretary JOHNSON. Correct.

Ms. JACKSON LEE. In my interpretation, the President's remarks over the years has been his lack of authority to confer immigration status or citizenship—my interpretation, but I think it would be documented by his words. You are telling us today that in the Executive Order you nor the President has done that.

Secretary JOHNSON. Deferred action does not grant legal status in this country.

Ms. JACKSON LEE. Or a pathway to citizenship.

Secretary JOHNSON. Or a green card or a pathway to citizenship.

Ms. JACKSON LEE. Let me move on, Mr. Secretary, to put into the record these words: "A comprehensive approach [to immigration reform]"—and that is in parens—"is long overdue, and I am confident that the President, myself, and others can find common ground to take care of this issue once and for all.'' Now, those were the words of Speaker Boehner, which I took literally, in 2012.

To date, this Congress has not placed—this House has not placed on the floor of the House one single immigration bill that responds to what I thought were welcoming words by the Speaker. We have not had an up-or-down vote.

In this committee, which I want to congratulate, the Chairman and the Ranking Member have worked in a bipartisan manner, my subcommittee Chairwoman and myself, and we have passed H.R. 1417, a border-security legislative initiative. It has never seen a day on the floor of the House to provide an up-or-down vote.

My questions and concerns would be our interpretation. President Reagan signed into law in 1986 a bill that many people tried to muffle their words but they use the word ''amnesty.'' I would make the argument that President Reagan saw a humanitarian crisis and decided to act. In the Phoenix case in 2012, Justice Roberts said that Presidents, in addition to the Executive Order, have a right to humanitarian relief.

So let me pursue this questioning regarding the DACA and the issue that this may work to cause border crosses as a result of this announcement.

Could you just quickly point out that DACA relief deals with existing persons here in the United States? One other aspect is to expand the time frame from 2 to 3 years. Could you quickly answer that?

Why don't I just give you this other question so that we won't be delayed with respect to the other question?

I have always thought Secure Communities have had a legal and political issue. You have streamlined Secure Communities. Let me say that my law enforcement officers locally have said it is problematic. So, in your prioritization of terrorists and others, you have streamlined that.

I would like to also indicate in your new facility that I am very interested in in Dilley, Texas, that it will be accommodating and with the right kinds of resources for family and children.

If you would answer those questions, Mr. Secretary.

Secretary JOHNSON. Yes, ma'am.

The current DACA program is for those who have been here since June 2007, which is almost 7 years—over 7 years. You have to have been here over 7 years, come here under age 16, and have been born after 1981.

We revised the criteria by rolling back the cut-off from 2007 to 2010, we removed the birthday limitation from post-1981 to any time, and we have made the eligibility for the temporary period 3 years instead of 2 years.

With regard to the Dilley facility that we are opening up, I have sent my own staff, my own lawyers, down there to ensure that the conditions are adequate for family units. That is something that I am committed to ensuring.

Ms. JACKSON LEE. Secure Communities that you have streamlined, which have really rounded up mothers and fathers and people who have are no threat to the United States of America.

Secretary JOHNSON. I support the goal of Secure Communities. The goal of Secure Communities is to get at criminals so they can be put in removal——

Ms. JACKSON LEE. Absolutely.

Secretary JOHNSON. The program, as you know, was becoming legally and politically controversial, mayors and Governors signing laws and executive orders prohibiting their law enforcement from working with ours on this. So I want to fresh start so that we can better enforce public safety and removing criminals.

Ms. JACKSON LEE. I thank you.

Mr. Chairman, as I yield back, I just want to say that, in an article in our local newspaper, a mother who had used a nanny for a number of years who had been in this country for 13 years, dependent, as many mothers across America are, on child care in the house, she was celebrating—not politically, Democrats, Republicans—the opportunity for her nanny to become in some way statused to stay in this country and to do good work and to protect her children.

I yield back.

Chairman MCCAUL. The Chairman recognizes Mr. Rogers from Alabama.

Mr. ROGERS. Thank you, Chairman.

Thank you, Mr. Johnson, for your service and for being here.

Earlier this year, you testified before this committee when we had a bunch of younger people coming across the border illegally. During that hearing, I asked you, when we were talking about the reason why they wouldn't be removed within 24 hours like we do adult illegal aliens coming across the border, you made the point of saying, statutorily, the Government is required to allow these children to go through or these younger people to go through a hearing process and that that had to be complied with.

My inquiry to you was: Aren't these exigent circumstances? You said yes. I said, well, under those circumstances, can't the President write an Executive Order that would allow you to go ahead and remove those younger people like we do adults? You said the President doesn't have that authority to ignore a statute by Executive Order.

Isn't it true that our current statutory law requires that these people that are covered under this Executive Order be removed from the country?

Secretary JOHNSON. I recall that exchange, and I recall that the particular words, "extraordinary circumstances" or "exigent circumstances," whatever was in the law, could not be read as broadly as to permit voluntary departure and basically obviate the entire statute. That was the reading of the statute that I had at the time.

I do not believe, to the extent this is your question, that that is inconsistent with anything we have done and announced week before last.

Mr. ROGERS. I disagree with you. The statue is very clear at present that these illegals who are in this country are to be removed once they are located.

My next question: You talked about how the people are going to be defined under this Executive Order, by being here a certain number of years or the age or whatever. How do you determine that how they are presenting themselves is accurate?

For example, if they say, "I have been here 7 years," how do you get them to prove it, and how do you know that the way they prove it is valid?

For example, if they say, "Well, I have been living at this address for the last 7 years, and here is the power bill over that period of time," and the power bill is in another person's name, and they say, "Look, but I rent from that person," and that person says, "Oh, yeah," and it is a complete fabrication, how do you prove the residency is accurate when they present themselves to you?

Secretary JOHNSON. Good question. The onus will be on the applicant to demonstrate that they have lived in this country continuously for the 5-year period. So the onus is on the applicant to come forward with something that satisfies the immigration officer, the examining officer, that they have, in fact, lived in this country.

I do not believe that that will be as simple as, you know, "Take my word for it." There will have to be some sort of documented proof. That will be developed in the implementation process by CIS.

Mr. ROGERS. Well, I think you acknowledged from an earlier question, this is an area that is going to be wrought with fraud. All sorts of lies and exploitation are going to be driven to this point. I think it is going to be impossible for you all to be able to determine who, in fact, qualifies under this very broad and illegal Executive Order.

Let me ask you this question: Do you think that the people that are going to fall into this category are going to be able to draw Medicare and Social Security and other public benefits?

Secretary JOHNSON. People who qualify for deferred action are lawfully present, but they do not have a lawful status like lawful permanent resident or citizen. One of the virtues, I think, of accountability is you give people a work authorization and then they pay taxes on the books. Part of the taxes they would pay, as I understand it, would be a deduction for Social Security.

Mr. ROGERS. So the answer is, yes, they will be able to qualify——

Secretary JOHNSON. They will not be eligible for public benefits of the type that most people would receive——

Mr. ROGERS. But Medicare and Social Security, they would.

Secretary JOHNSON. You would generally, as I understand it, be eligible, if you are around long enough, to get back what you put in, what you invested originally, but not——

Mr. ROGERS. So the answer is yes.

Secretary JOHNSON [continuing]. The normal public benefits we would think of.

Mr. ROGERS. Well, participating in Medicare and Social Security, both of which are struggling financially through solvency, to have this added burden I think is irresponsible.

Now, you made a point about being given documentation for a work permit. Is that accurate? This program will issue affirmatively a document to an illegal saying they have a legal status of some sort?

Secretary JOHNSON. As a separate matter, those who apply for deferred action can also apply for a work authorization, which is not a green card. It is a separate form of work authorization that the Secretary of Homeland Security has the authority to provide.

Mr. ROGERS. But it will be a legal status of some sort.

Secretary JOHNSON. They can be considered lawfully present in the country, just like the DACA kids.

Mr. ROGERS. Do you know how much it will cost for the Department of Homeland Security to establish and carry out that program of providing that documentation? How expensive will it be for you?

Secretary JOHNSON. Well, the program will be fee-driven. An applicant has to pay a fee. I believe that we are contemplating that the fee be $460 per applicant, which is what it is for DACA. USCIS is a fee-based organization. It pays for itself.

Mr. ROGERS. Great. Thank you very much.

I yield back.

Chairman McCAUL. Mr. Keating from Massachusetts.

Mr. KEATING. Thank you, Mr. Chairman. Thank you for having the hearing.

Thank you, Mr. Secretary.

The title of today's hearing is "Open Borders: The Impact of Presidential Amnesty on Border Security."

Before this hearing gets too far, let me be very direct, Mr. Secretary. Is this amnesty?

Secretary JOHNSON. No. No, in my judgment.

Mr. KEATING. Not legally, and is it even functionally amnesty?

Secretary JOHNSON. The current situation amounts to amnesty. We want people to be accountable, to come out of the shadows, get on the books, and pay taxes for the 3-year period of deferred action.

Mr. KEATING. Thank you, Mr. Secretary.

I have another question. Does this represent a permanent solution, this Executive Action, in your opinion?

Secretary JOHNSON. No.

Let me say again, I would welcome the opportunity to work with the Members of this committee who I know are interested in immigration reform on both sides of the aisle. Unfortunately, since I have been in office, we have not had a willing partner in the House of Representatives.

But I continue to want to work with Members of this committee and Members of the House and Members of the Congress on a comprehensive immigration reform piece of legislation. Because you are correct; this is not a permanent solution. But it is in our existing legal authority to issue to fix the broken system, and we feel that we had no choice.

Mr. KEATING. Mr. Secretary, General Barry McCaffrey served as a witness during a border-security hearing before this committee in the last Congress, and he unequivocally said that the lack of comprehensive immigration reform is a direct threat to our National security.

Would you comment on that, please?

Secretary JOHNSON. Part of comprehensive immigration reform that was passed by the Senate enhanced border security—more resources, more technology, more surveillance. I support that, and I agree with that. I am hoping that the Congress will act on our pending request for added border security on the Southwest Border in response to last summer's spike.

Border security is integral to National security. So I agree with that, sir.

Mr. KEATING. Okay.

I know that there are some limitations on what you can say, and most of the Members of this committee have been briefed in a Classified manner on this issue. But can you enlighten us and the members of the public, too, as to some of the means that have been implemented in terms of border security, particularly use of satellites to a greater extent and use of military assets that we have that we no longer need that can be surplussed and used on the border?

Secretary JOHNSON. When I go down to the border, the Southern Border, and I talk to our Border Patrol about what they need, they almost always tell me more vehicles, more surveillance, more technology.

We are moving in the direction of a risk-based strategy to border security, homeland security, aviation security, because we now have the capability to surveil high-risk areas of the border. So we need to continue in that direction. We need more technology. That includes aerial surveillance as well as mobile surveillance on the ground and a number of other things.

We have made considerable investments, Congressman, over the last 15 years, which has shown some good results, but I believe that we can do better and we should continue to do better in this regard.

Mr. KEATING. I am disappointed we do not have a vote in the House at this stage on the Senate bill or a bill like that.

But let me ask you another question, my last question. That is, there was some discussion by Members that asked you questions in terms of your ability to send people back. Can you be clear about your fiscal resources to do that right now, what you are capable of? Are you capable of sending everyone back?

If we are really serious about this, how much do we need to fund your agency so that we can do what the Members of this committee are asking you to do?

Secretary JOHNSON. Well, the answer to that question is reflected in our current budget request.

Let me say this. I know that there are some contemplating some form of short-term CR for the Department of Homeland Security to get us to March. That is, in my judgment, a very bad idea for Homeland Security, because during that period of a CR we cannot engage in new starts. We have some Homeland Security priorities that need to be funded now.

For example, we are back in a Presidential election cycle. I cannot hire new Secret Service agents until I get an appropriations bill passed by this Congress, not another CR for a couple of months. I cannot continue to fund our enhanced detention capability in Texas with another CR that gets me to March.

I need the help of Congress to support and build upon border security, which I believe all of you support. So I am urging that we act on our current appropriations request now for the purpose and for the sake of border security and homeland security.

Mr. KEATING. Thank you, Mr. Secretary, for those direct answers.

I yield back.

Chairman McCAUL. The Chairman recognizes Mrs. Miller from Michigan.

Mrs. MILLER. Thank you very much, Mr. Chairman.

Good morning, Mr. Secretary. I appreciate your attendance here this morning.

Obviously, there is a huge divide, certainly in Congress and I think out there in the heartland as well, about whether or not this is a Constitutional overreach by the President.

Just listening to your testimony and I read through your testimony last night and hearing the answers to some of the questions, you obviously had a very heavy, heavy, heavy reliance on the OLC's opinion, their 33-page opinion that they issued in here through Mr. Holder's Department of Justice.

I wrote a note when you said that they were very, very thorough, but yet it seems to me that the questions that you did ask them were specifically tailored. The three questions that you asked the OLC were very specific in nature. Perhaps there were some questions that you could have asked that you did not.

But I would just—could you tell us the process in which you actually asked these three specific questions of the OLC? Because I see some of the States are going to be suing. I am sure this is going to be a question that is probably determined by the courts, and your department had such a heavy reliance on them.

Secretary JOHNSON. Well, I know from my days at the Department of Defense, and now, that the way we typically work with OLC is to put to them specific questions. Do we have the authority to do X? Do we have the authority to target XYZ military objective, for example? So we developed the two or three most significant questions that would be part of this Executive Action package to be put to OLC for them to consider. They came back with this very thorough opinion. I will say that, as a lawyer myself, and as someone who has been a lawyer for a Government agency, I am fully comfortable with what is in here because I know that at the end of the day I am going to have to be the one here to defend it.

Mrs. MILLER. Well, if I could, in 2012, when this administration created the DACA policy, there is nothing that we could find of any opinion from the OLC regarding that. It just would seem to be sort of a glaring oversight from there. Is there such a memo? If there is such a memo, I guess we would like to see that.

Secretary JOHNSON. I can only speak to 2014, and we wanted to be thorough, so——

Mrs. MILLER. But certainly as you were looking at this you would have asked OLC, was there ever a memo in regards to DACA? You never asked that question?

Secretary JOHNSON. I am not aware of one. Based on everything I have asked and been told, I am not aware of one. I have not seen one. I wanted to be thorough this time around, though.

Mrs. MILLER. Yeah. We think there was a glaring omission about that as well. Again, in regards to the OLC, and this will be determined in the courts, I think, since, I mean, I certainly believe this was a Constitutional overreach by this administration. As I say, it appears that some of the States are going to court on that.

I was also taking notes here, Secretary, as you mentioned about the fees, a $460 fee. I did some quick math, it is probably not right, but times 4 million, $1.84 billion. I am just wondering because, again, the OLC is saying you need to do it, guarantee it in an individualized case-by-case review, is what they are saying. So some of the questions even this morning were talking about the limited amount of resources that you have.

So you are going to do 4 million case-by-case reviews. How in the world are you going to pay for this? I mean, really, is that going to be enough? I mean, right now you have a couple of dozen field stations. I am not quite sure of the mechanics of actually doing a case-by-case review. I think that will be such an important, critical component for the Department so that you are not just doing a free-for-all and just rubber stamping and really taking a look at all of this. So how do you envision that all unfolding as you do a case-by-case review of over 4 million individuals?

Secretary JOHNSON. Well, we have an implementation period, a start-up time of 6 months. DACA was 60 days. We determined that for this one we needed 6 months to make sure that we get it right. We know from the DACA experience that the program, if the fee is set at the right level, will pay for itself. So the fee for DACA was $460 per applicant, and that is the same fee that we will be charging here.

With regard to the number 4 million, let me say this: 4.1 million is the estimated potential class of those who would be eligible. Not all of those will come forward, as the DACA experience shows. The estimated potential class of DACA kids is over a million, but the number of those who are actually enrolled is somewhere about 600,000 or 700,000. Then of those who come forward, some will not qualify because they didn't survive the background check or for some other reason; they didn't establish proof of living here for 5 years. So the number 4.1 is the estimate of the total potential class, but not all of those will be enrolled in the program.

Mrs. MILLER. Thank you very much. I think my time has expired here.

Thank you, Mr. Chairman,

Chairman MCCAUL. Thank you.

The Chairman recognizes Mr. Barber from Arizona.

Mr. BARBER. Thank you, Mr. Chairman, for convening this hearing.

Thank you, Mr. Secretary, for being with us today. I want to start by just saying how much I appreciate, and I think I am joined by other Members on both sides of the aisle of this committee, how much I appreciate the forthrightness with which you approach the questions and the concerns that we have and the leadership you have provided to the Department over almost the last year.

As you know, Mr. Secretary, you visited my district within a month of your appointment, your confirmation, and you saw first-hand and you heard first-hand from people who live along the border, work along the border, what their main issue is. They are concerned about people coming here illegally seeking work, but they are even more concerned about the traffic of drug smugglers and the potential violence that comes with them.

That is one of the reasons I cosponsored, along with many Members of this committee, the Border Security Results Act, which passed unanimously here—it is important to stress unanimously in this committee—and has yet to be brought to the floor. I also cosponsored with almost 200 other Members H.R. 15, a bipartisan bill that would include the Border Security Results Act and the immigration provisions of the Senate bill which bipartisan passed the Senate.

I have said from Day 1 that Congress needs to act, and we have failed in our responsibility to act to secure the border and to fix the broken immigration system. Because of that failure, unfortunately Executive Action has been taken. I believe it should be done in concert with Congress, but we have failed on our side of the bargain. I fully support the McCain-Flake bill which is sitting there ready for us to take up.

Could you, Mr. Secretary, initially my first question is, could you address how the Executive Action comports with the McCain-Flake bill, particularly as it regards both border security and immigration? I know it is not comprehensive, it can't be. But to what extent was that bill a template for action that can be taken and must be taken to secure the border and to fix the system?

Secretary JOHNSON. Well, the Executive Actions that we have taken are no substitute for S. 744, which does a number of things, including an earned path to citizenship. That is what is contemplated in the bill. We do not have Executive authority to provide an earned path to citizenship. We do have Executive authority to provide deferred action for those who have been here for years, similar to the bill, who have not committed any crimes and who have basically become integrated members of the American society, to offer them the opportunity to be accountable. That is not citizenship. That is not lawful permanent residence. It is simply you are deemed lawfully present in the country for a period of time.

We also are, through Executive Actions, enhancing border security in a number of ways. But, again, border security is something that is not cost-free. So we have reprioritized recent illegal entrants, which we plainly have the authority to do, but I need help with resources. I need help on the Southern Border in Arizona, in Texas, New Mexico, for added detention capability, added surveillance capability, added vehicles, added equipment, and I am hoping the Congress will support me on that.

I received your letter about the Eastern Border along Arizona, and I plan to, if you will have me, come back early next year to Arizona. I owe the ranchers another visit. I want to come back to Arizona now with the benefit of a year's experience in the job to talk more about border security and see what we can do.

Mr. BARBER. I appreciate your willingness to come back and look forward to having you there.

Let me just focus in my remaining time on the issue of border security. I think the answers, from my experience, having worked on this issue for Congresswoman Giffords and in my own right, is pretty straightforward: Border Patrol Agents at the border, not 10, 15, 20 miles back under the defense-in-depth strategy, which I think has failed in that area; more horse patrols in the rugged territory; aerostats that will allow us to have radar looking down into the mountains to see where the smugglers are coming from; more mobile surveillance systems at the border. I hope that your task force that you have established, the western task force, will look at these strategic options and include stakeholders, such as ranchers, business people, residents of the communities there, as well as others, to make sure we get it right going forward. Thank you.

Secretary JOHNSON. Congressman, I can affirm for you, when I talk to the Border Patrol myself the one thing they mention always, aerostats. So I believe that is a border security priority.

Mr. BARBER. Thank you, Mr. Secretary.

Thank you, Mr. Chairman. I yield back.

Chairman McCAUL. The Chairman recognizes the gentleman from South Carolina, Mr. Duncan.

Mr. DUNCAN. Thank you, Mr. Chairman. Thanks for holding this hearing.

It comes as no surprise that I disagree with the President and what he has done with this Executive Action. It is not as much the issue of immigration and dealing with undocumented workers as it is what he actually did. I think he crossed a line with the Constitutional separation of powers. But I hear a lot of doublespeak in his speech and in the words that I have heard today. I will give you an example. The President said in his November 20 speech about this unconstitutional Executive Action that, ''Undocumented workers broke our immigration laws, and I believe that they must be held accountable.'' That is directly from his speech. ''Felons, not families. Criminals, not children. Gang members, not a mom who is working hard to provide for her kids. We will prioritize, just like law enforcement does every day.''

But in *The Hill* publication, May 2014, it documented that DHS released 68,000 illegal immigrants with criminal convictions. ''Immigration and Customs Enforcement officials last year released 68,000 illegal immigrants with criminal convictions.'' That comes from an end-of-year ''Weekly Departures and Detentions Report.'' How do you reconcile, Mr. Secretary, what the President said with the actions of the agency?

Secretary JOHNSON. Well, with regard to those who are released from immigration detention, this is something I have worked on myself. First of all, there is a Supreme Court case, *Zadvydas* v. *Davis,* which you may have heard of, which mandates that after 6 months if the person is not going to be repatriated in the foreseeable future, we have to let them go unless——

Mr. DUNCAN. So why aren't we repatriating these people?

Secretary JOHNSON. Well, that is something that requires a willing partner on the other end, which I have had conversations with the State Department about to further encourage countries to take these people back faster. But if I may——

Mr. DUNCAN. We had a hearing in the Foreign Affairs Committee about that last week, and countries should take these. I mean, they are required to take these back. I didn't mean to interrupt you.

Secretary JOHNSON. If I could finish my sentence, yes, thank you. So a number of releases are mandated by law and Supreme Court jurisprudence. A number of releases are ordered by an immigration judge.

With regard to the instances where an immigration official who works for me releases somebody with a criminal record, what I have recently directed is that the approval for that be at a higher level of the ICE field officer. I want to know that we are applying a consistent standard to those circumstances because they may jeopardize public safety. I have also directed that a person should not be released because of reasons for fiscal constraint, which is what we faced when we had sequestration in fiscal year 2013. We will find a way to pay for it if we believe somebody should not be released for reasons of public safety.

Mr. DUNCAN. I think some reports came out, Mr. Secretary, that sequestration really had nothing to do with the release of folks last year. I could go back and find the documents.

Let me ask you this. At the end of the year of 2014, how many criminal aliens have been released? What will your year-end ''Weekly Departures and Detention Report'' show for 2014?

Secretary JOHNSON. I believe it is less than fiscal year 2013. Fiscal year 2013, I believe, was 36,000. I think the number for fiscal year 2030 will be about 30,000, and I think it should be lower.

Mr. DUNCAN. So about 30,000, plus or minus, criminal aliens have been released?

Secretary JOHNSON. Pursuant to legal requirements, orders of a judge, I believe it should be lower, which is why I have enhanced the approval authority. I have raised the approval authority for that.

Mr. DUNCAN. I think one of the biggest problems with getting any kind of immigration issues passed through the United States Congress is a lack of trust of the American people in the administration to enforce the laws. They have told me, and I know my colleagues have heard it on both sides of the aisle, why would you pass another law when the administration fails to enforce the current laws that are on the books? Why pass another one that is not going to be enforced either?

Then you hear about 68,000 criminal illegal aliens that have been released, that further erodes the trust of the American people. The American people want to see border security. They want to see deportations. They want to see enforcement of the law. When they see that 50 percent, 50 percent, 49 percent I will give you that, of the illegals in this country are visa overstays, these are people that we are not chasing a footprint in the desert. We know who they are. We have got their name. They have had an interview at a consulate or an embassy. They came here on a visa. We know who they are. That is low-hanging fruit for enforcement.

So I ask you this: How many of the visa overstays are granted immunity through the President's action? Any?

Secretary JOHNSON. Off-hand I don't know. I don't know the answer to that. Congressman, I will say this, though. I would like to see this Congress pass a bill. I would like to work with Congress on passing a bill. The President has said that would be his preference. The problem is we have no partner in Congress.

Mr. DUNCAN. I think Congress can pass a bill when the American people start regaining trust in the administration to actually do their job and enforce the laws that are already on the books. I yield back.

Chairman MCCAUL. Chairman recognizes Mr. O'Rourke from Texas.

Mr. O'ROURKE. Thank you, Mr. Chairman.

Mr. Secretary, I want to begin by thanking you for your accountability. You mentioned that you have been before Congress 13 times in the 12 months you have been here, 5 times before this committee. Your responsiveness to our requests and our questions and your commitment to transparency, I think there is a long way to go still within the Department, but in the last 12 months we have seen more transparency than we have seen in years, and so I really appreciate that.

Through you I want to thank the President for this very difficult decision that he made, a very imperfect decision by its very nature, a temporary way to address some of the fundamental problems that require a legislative response. But I think the status quo is untenable. As you and others have said, it amounted to effective amnesty, and we are going to gain some accountability, and we are going to bring families and people who are working in our communities out of the shadows.

In a community like mine, El Paso, where 25 percent of the population are immigrants, more than 40 percent of the kids who live in my community are raised by parents who are immigrants, this is going to be a boon. It is going to make us more secure, a city that is already the safest city in America today, and I tell people not in spite of the number of immigrants who there, but in large part because of them. So on behalf of the people I represent, I want to thank you and I want to thank the President.

I do, however, want to address an issue that Congressmen Smith and Duncan brought up, and that is the release of convicted criminals. Senator Cornyn and I wrote a letter to ICE and have yet to receive a response, almost a month ago, with important questions about the status of those who have been released, where they are, how we improve our working with local law enforcement so that our police and sheriff's departments know when these criminals are released and are able to track them and account for them. So I would just appreciate your commitment to getting me and Senator Cornyn a response to that.

Secretary JOHNSON. One of the things I have directed when it comes to releases of those with criminal records is that we notify local law enforcement when that happens. I think that should be done. I will personally look for your letter, from you and Senator Cornyn, and make sure it is responded to promptly if it hasn't been already.

Mr. O'ROURKE. Thank you.

Secretary JOHNSON. But I will look to make sure. We have a general rule of responding within 14 days to Members of Congress.

Mr. O'ROURKE. Mr. Secretary, I would like to make a point and try to turn it into a question about the President's response to our immigration system thus far. I feel like there has been this implicit political bargain where there is going to be stepped-up enforcement and deportations. I believe this President has deported more people from this country than any President prior, 2 million at this point, and unfortunately in many cases that is breaking up families, which this current action I think will help reduce. I think the bargain was that in return we were going to be able to gain the trust of both parties in Congress and be able to pass meaningful immigration reform. That obviously has not happened.

So I am concerned about some comments that you have made and the President has made about stepping up border security, about prioritizing the deportation of recent arrivals. I spent some time in Artesia, the family detention center there, which really has effectively become a deportation machine. I think we are short-cutting due process, and I think we threaten to return families and have returned families and children into some very dangerous situations. Certainly there are those who should be deported, but certainly there are those who qualify for asylum in our country, and I think we need to honor that process. So when you mentioned the facility in Dilley, Texas, I want to make sure in our effort to satisfy security concerns we don't shorten due process for those.

Then when it comes to border security, you and others have said the border has never been more secure. We are spending $18 billion a year, 20,000 Border Patrol Agents. In the El Paso Sector, the average agent apprehends 4.5 people a year, not in a week, not in a month, but for the entire year. So when we talk about stepping up border enforcement and this Southern Border Campaign Strategy, I would like to know what that means for my community. Is that simply repositioning resources along the border, as my colleague Congressman Barber said, moving the Border Patrol up to the line of the border instead of being set back, or are you asking for ultimately more Border Patrol Agents, more walls, more of these militarization measures, which I think show us that we have a problem with diminishing returns right now. You mentioned 1.6 million apprehended in 2000, not even 500,000 this year. At what point do we have enough security on the border?

Secretary JOHNSON. First of all, I have been to Artesia myself. That facility there, it is being closed. I want to make sure that we have adequate ability for effective attorney-client communications. We made some enhancements there, but it is being closed in lieu of a larger facility in Dilley, Texas, as I mentioned earlier. I want to make sure that the conditions of detention there are adequate and meet the appropriate standards.

I believe that added detention capability on the Southern Border, and some disagree with me, is essential to border security, and it is essential to border security going forward in the future. It is correct that apprehensions are way down from where they were 15 years ago, resources are way up. But I believe we can do better. So I am not going to sit here and declare we have a secure border. We can do better. I think we know how to do better. The Congress and the Executive branch together can spend the time and effort to do better on border security. We have made great strides, but there is more to do.

Our Southern Border campaign plan is not simply repositioning assets. It is to bring a more strategic, consolidated approach toward how we secure our border, bringing to bear the assets across my Department, not in a stovepipe fashion, but in a more coordinated way, region by region, so that there is one person in the Southwest who is responsible for bringing to bear all of the assets of my Department on border security in Arizona, New Mexico, and in Texas.

Chairman McCAUL. The gentleman's time has expired.

The Chairman now recognizes the incoming Chairman of Government Reform and Oversight. Congratulations. Mr. Chaffetz.

Mr. CHAFFETZ. Thank you. I thank the Chairman for holding this hearing.

Mr. Secretary, I thank you for being here. I hope you are able to convey the love and gratitude for the men and women who serve in the Customs and Border Patrol, the ICE Agents who put their lives on the line every day for this country. We thank them for their service.

My question for you, Mr. Secretary, is: What do you say to someone who believes the President took action to change the law?

Secretary JOHNSON. We did not change the law. We acted within the law.

Mr. CHAFFETZ. Can you play the clip?

This is from November 25. This is the President in Nevada talking about this.

[Video shown. President Obama: "But what you are not paying attention to is the fact that I just took an action to change the law."]

Mr. CHAFFETZ. So you say he didn't change the law, but the President says he changed the law.

Secretary JOHNSON. We acted within existing law. We acted within our existing legal authority. Listen, I have been a lawyer 30 years. Somebody plays me an eight-word excerpt from a broader speech, I know to be suspicious. Okay? That was very nice.

Mr. CHAFFETZ. It says, I am going to read it back, "Now, you are absolutely right that there have been a significant number of deportations. That is true. But what you are not paying attention to is the fact I just took action to change the law.'" So that is point No. 1.

Point No. 2, the way the change in the law works, and he goes on. He is pretty clear, and he is the President of the United States. This is why we have a hard time believing that Homeland Security is doing the right thing. I think the gentleman from South Carolina made a very good point.

Let me move to something else real quickly. You and I had an interaction the last time you were here about these four people with ties to a terrorist organization were caught illegally crossing the border into Texas in September. You said they would be deported. Did you deport them?

Secretary JOHNSON. No, not at this point.

Mr. CHAFFETZ. What is the disposition of those four people?

Secretary JOHNSON. Two are detained. The two others were released by the judge. Not my preference. They were released by the judge, and they fled to Canada, and they are seeking asylum in Canada.

Mr. CHAFFETZ. So you told the world that you were going to deport these four people with ties to a terrorist organization. That is not what happened. Two of them were released——

Secretary JOHNSON. They are in deportation proceedings. An immigration judge released two of the four, and they fled to Canada. My intent is that they be deported, but two of them are in Canada seeking asylum.

Mr. CHAFFETZ. Where did these two, where were they anticipated going, and where did they actually go?

Secretary JOHNSON. I am not sure of their exact whereabouts, sir.

Mr. CHAFFETZ. But they are currently being held in Canada?

Secretary JOHNSON. That is my understanding.

Mr. CHAFFETZ. Are you going to ask that they be brought back to the United States?

Secretary JOHNSON. I don't generally get involved in individual immigration cases.

Mr. CHAFFETZ. But these people had ties to a terrorist organization.

Secretary JOHNSON. I think, as we talked about this last time, there is some question about whether their affiliation is with what one should consider a terrorist organization.

Mr. CHAFFETZ. It is a terrorist organization designated by the State Department, correct?

Secretary JOHNSON. They are or were a member of the Kurdish Workers Party.

Mr. CHAFFETZ. That is designated by the State Department as a terrorist organization, correct?

Secretary JOHNSON. I refer you to the State Department.

Mr. CHAFFETZ. That is the accurate statement.

Mr. Secretary, this is the problem, you come and you say, you tell the world that you are going to deport these four people tied to terror. These are terrorists. You don't. They get released. My understanding is they go to Arizona. They go to the State of Washington. They cross illegally into Canada. They each put up $25,000 bonds. Doesn't that beg a lot of questions about what you are doing in deporting criminals? These people have terrorist ties.

I am getting tired of the Democrats with this righteous indignation saying that we can't find a Congress we can work with. Well, the first 2 years of the Obama administration the Democrats had the House, the Senate, and the Presidency, and they did nothing on immigration. I sat on the subcommittee. They brought Stephen Colbert in to testify. That is how bad it was.

The country made a change. We actually passed an immigration bill. It was my bill. Nearly 390 people voted for it. It is as bipartisan as it gets. Worked on high-skilled immigrants. Dealt with family-based visas. Took the per-country cap from 7 percent to 15 percent. It went to the United States Senate under Harry Reid. It had nothing happen to it. Nothing.

So I want to continue to work with this administration. There is common ground that can be had. But the President and the record is clear. When they had the chance with the House, the Senate, and the Presidency, they didn't even introduce a bill into the committee, let alone bring it through the process.

I appreciate the time. Yield back.

Chairman MCCAUL. The Chairman recognizes Mr. Vela.

Ms. JACKSON LEE. Mr. Chairman, may I offer something into the record?

Chairman MCCAUL. Yes. The gentlelady is recognized.

Ms. JACKSON LEE. Thank you, Mr. Chairman. There are three articles or letters or statements emphasizing the approach of the

President in deporting felons and not families. One is from the National Immigrant Justice Center, dated December 2, 2014; from the American Immigration Lawyers Association, dated December 2, 2014; and from the Southern Border Communities Coalition and the ACLU, dated December 2, 2014. I ask unanimous consent to submit these statements into the record.

Chairman McCAUL. Without objection, so ordered.

[The information follows:]

STATEMENT OF MARY MEG McCARTHY, EXECUTIVE DIRECTOR, NATIONAL IMMIGRANT JUSTICE CENTER

DECEMBER 2, 2014

Chairman McCaul, Ranking Member Thompson, and Members of the Committee on Homeland Security: Drawing upon our vast experience working with children and families from Mexico and Central America, Heartland Alliance's National Immigrant Justice Center (NIJC) submits this testimony to demonstrate that the reason families and children are coming to the United States is to escape violence and is not related to the President's Executive Action. Pervasive violence and the absence of the rule of law in Central America drive migrants to the United States in search of safe haven.

While the President's Executive Action will provide security to millions of families with deep roots in the United States, unfortunately it puts those fleeing recent violence in Central America at greater risk. NIJC welcomes President Obama's recent announcement to expand eligibility for the Deferred Action for Childhood Arrivals (DACA) program and to extend eligibility for deferred action to parents of U.S. citizens and lawful permanent residents to allow them to contribute to our communities and economy. This temporary relief should allow the administration to refocus immigration enforcement on those who pose a National security threat or risk to public safety,[1] not those who come to our borders seeking refuge.

This testimony will discuss lessons learned from the arrivals of children and families from Central America during 2014, including the root causes of migration, the need for greater due process protections, and the need for improved accountability and oversight of the Department of Homeland Security's (DHS) border screening process.

NIJC is an NGO dedicated to safeguarding the rights of noncitizens. With offices in Chicago, Indiana, and Washington, DC, NIJC advocates for immigrants, refugees, asylum seekers, and survivors of human trafficking through direct legal representation, policy reform, impact litigation, and public education. NIJC and its network of 1,500 pro bono attorneys provide legal representation to approximately 10,000 noncitizens annually, including thousands of unaccompanied children. NIJC is the largest legal service provider for unaccompanied children detained in Illinois, conducting weekly legal screenings and legal rights presentations, which provide an overview of the child's legal rights and responsibilities in the immigration system, at nine Chicago-area shelters. Through our direct legal services, we have heard of the horrors that force children to leave their parents behind and make treacherous journeys in hope of finding refuge in the United States.

I. VIOLENCE FORCES CHILDREN AND FAMILIES TO FLEE CENTRAL AMERICA

Growing violence and danger in home countries is the primary reason children and families are fleeing their countries and seeking safety in the United States. The majority of these new arrivals are from the Northern Triangle countries of El Salvador, Guatemala, and Honduras, are among the most dangerous countries in the world, particularly for women and children. In 2011, El Salvador had the highest rate of gender-motivated killing of women in the world, followed by Guatemala (third-highest) and Honduras (sixth-highest).[2] In addition, children in these coun-

---

[1] Memorandum from Secretary Jeh Johnson, "Policies for the Apprehension, Detention, and Removal of Undocumented Immigrants," Nov. 20, 2014, *http://www.dhs.gov/sites/default/files/publications/14\1120\memo\prosecutorial\discretion.pdf.*

[2] Geneva Declaration on Armed Violence and Development, *Global Burden of Armed Violence 2011,* Oct. 2011, *http://www.genevadeclaration.org/fileadmin/docs/GBAV2/GBAV2011\-CH4\rev.pdf.*

tries face pervasive violence, persecution, and abuse.[3] El Salvador led the world in child murders in 2012 with 27 children murdered per 100,000 population.[4] Overall, the region has the highest rate of child homicides in the world.[5]

''One of those children is Alex, a 13-year-old boy and NIJC client who was murdered for refusing to join a gang in Guatemala. A year after his murder, his friend Oscar (pseudonym) fled to the United States to escape gang violence. For the past two years, the same gang that killed Alex had been threatening to kill Oscar if he did not join the gang. Initially, the gang tried to force Oscar to do things he did not want to do, like use drugs. As time went on, their efforts to force Oscar to join the gang escalated, but Oscar could not go to the police for help because the gang threatened to kill his family. Oscar decided to leave after a friend told him that the gang had set a date and time to kill him. He came to the United States to seek refuge with his father, who has lived in the United States for nearly 10 years.''

Oscar is one of many children targeted by gangs who cannot obtain police protection because violence in these countries is perpetrated with impunity. For instance, over the past 3 years, 48,947 people were murdered in the Northern Triangle, where the total population is just over 30 million inhabitants. Countries achieved convictions in 2,295 of those homicide cases, representing a regional impunity rate of 95 percent for homicides over that 3-year period.[6] In 2012, Honduras had the highest homicide rate in the world with 90.4 homicides per 100,000, El Salvador had the fourth-highest homicide rate with 41.2 homicides per 100,000, and Guatemala had the fifth-highest homicide rate with 40 homicides per 100,000.[7] Alliances between drug-trafficking organizations and local gangs have increased the efficiency and frequency of violence in this region.[8] The DHS's own statistical analysis has shown that children and families are fleeing the countries in Latin American with the highest rates of homicides and the most dangerous security conditions.[9] Additionally, impoverished Latin American countries with lower rates of violence and homicide, such as Nicaragua, are not sending large numbers of children.[10]

II. CHILDREN AND FAMILIES FLEEING VIOLENCE ARE NOT INCLUDED IN THE PRESIDENT'S EXECUTIVE ACTION

Central American migration patterns are not tied to U.S. immigration policy making. The relief provided by DACA is unavailable to anyone who has entered the United States since January 1, 2010. The qualifications for DACA, whether under the 2012 directive or the more recent November 20, 2014 announcement, require continuous residence in the United States for at least 5 years.[11] Historic trends fur-

---

[3] See e.g., Kids in Need of Defense (KIND)/Center for Gender and Refugee Studies (CGRS), *A Treacherous Journey: Child Migrants Navigating the U.S. Immigration System*, http://www.usccb.org/about/migration-policy/upload/Mission-To-Central-America-FINAL-2.pdf; U.S. Conference of Catholic Bishops (USCCB), *Mission to Central America: The Flight of Unaccompanied Children to the United States*, 2014, http://www.usccb.org/about/migration-policy/upload/Mission-To-Central-America-FINAL-2.pdf; Women's Refugee Commission, *Forced from Home: The Lost Boys and Girls of Central America*, 2012, http://womensrefugeecommission.org/forced-from-home-press-kit; United Nations High Commissioner for Refugees (UNHCR), *Children on the Run*, 2014, http://www.unhcrwashington.org/children/reports.

[4] United Nations International Children's Emergency Fund (UNICEF), *Hidden in Plain Sight: A statistical analysis of violence against children*, Sept. 2014, http://files.unicef.org/publications/files/Hidden\in\plain\sight\statistical\analysis\EN\3\Sept\2014.pdf, p. 36.

[5] Id.

[6] Chavez, S. & Avalos, J., *The Northern Triangle: The Countries That Don't Cry for Their Dead*, INSIGHT CRIME—ORGANIZED CRIME IN THE AMERICAS, April 2014, http://www.insightcrime.org/news-analysis/the-northern-triangle-the-countries-that-dont-cry-for-their-dead.

[7] United Nations Office on Drugs and Crime (UNODC), *Global Study on Homicide*, 2013, http://www.unodc.org/documents/gsh/pdfs/2014\GLOBAL\HOMICIDE\BOOK\web.pdf.

[8] U.S. Conference of Catholic Bishops (USCCB), *Mission to Central America: The Flight of Unaccompanied Children in the United States*, p. 4, November 2013, http://www.usccb.org/about/migration-policy/upload/Mission-To-Central-America-FINAL-2.pdf.

[9] See Tom K. Wong, *Statistical Analysis Shows that Violence, Not Deferred Action, Is Behind the Surge of Unaccompanied Children Crossing the Border*, CENTER FOR AMERICAN PROGRESS, 2014, https://www.americanprogress.org/issues/immigration/news/2014/07/08/93370/statistical-analysis-shows-that-violence-not-deferred-action-is-behind-the-surge-of-unaccompanied-children-crossing-the-border.

[10] Id.

[11] U.S. Citizenship and Immigration Services, *Consideration of Deferred Action for Childhood Arrivals (DACA)*, October 2014, http://www.uscis.gov/humanitarian/consideration-deferred-action-childhood-arrivals-daca; Memo from DHS Secretary Jeh Johnson, Nov. 20, 2014, *Exercising Prosecutorial Discretion with Respect to Individuals Who Came to the United States as Children*

ther corroborate this argument. The increase in child migration to the United States began in October 2011, more than 6 months prior to President Obama's announcement of the DACA program. Furthermore, a recent Federal court decision cited a steady increase over the past 8 years in the number of individuals with prior removal orders expressing a fear of persecution.[12]

If a perceived change in immigration policy was fueling the current migration, there would be comparable numbers of immigrant children from other regional countries besides El Salvador, Guatemala, and Honduras, but this has not been the case. In addition, the United States is not the only country seeing an increase in refugees from these three countries. The United Nations High Commissioner for Refugees (UNHCR) has documented a 712 percent increase in the number of asylum applications from Salvadoran, Honduran, and Guatemalan citizens to Mexico, Panama, Nicaragua, Costa Rica, and Belize from 2008 to 2013.[13] These numbers demonstrate that the current crisis is a regional problem caused by country conditions in the sending countries, rather than a perceived change in immigration policies in the United States.

III. CUSTOMS AND BORDER PROTECTION NEEDS GREATER OVERSIGHT AND ACCOUNTABILITY

NIJC and its partners have documented reports of abuses by Customs and Border Protection (CBP) for years, most recently in two civil rights complaints on abuse of children in CBP custody and the unjust deportation of individuals with fear of persecution in their home countries. These complaints demonstrate the need for greater oversight and accountability of CBP.

In June of 2014, NIJC and several partner organizations filed a mass complaint on behalf of 116 children who were abused and mistreated while in CBP custody.[14] The complaint documents how CBP agents verbally and physically abused children in custody, denied access to necessary medical care to children as young as 5 months old, confiscated and withheld legal documents and personal belongs, and strip-searched and shackled children in three-point restraints during transport.

"D.G. is a 16-year-old girl who fled to the United States from Central America. Shortly after CBP arrested her, officials mocked her and asked her why she did not ask the Mexicans for help. When they searched her, officials violently spread her legs and touched her genital areas forcefully, making her scream. D.G. was detained with both children and adults. She describes the holding cell as ice-cold and filthy, and says the bright fluorescent lights were left on all day and night. D.G. became ill while in CBP custody, but when she asked to see a doctor, officials told her it was "not their fault" that she was sick and ignored her. CBP officials did not return all of D.G.'s personal belongings when she was released."[15]

D.G. is one of many children whose abuse was documented in NIJC's complaint. These types of abuses occurred in clear violation of standards on the treatment of children and American values. The volume and consistency of the complaints overall indicates long-standing, systemic problems with CBP policy and practices that require increased training on working with children and improved oversight by independent entities.

In addition, NIJC and nine other organizations recently filed a civil rights complaint on behalf of nine men and women who were unjustly deported by CBP Officers to countries where they faced persecution.[16] Under the 1951 Convention Relat-

---

and with Respect to Certain Individuals Who Are the Parents of U.S. Citizens or Permanent Residents, http://www.dhs.gov/sites/default/files/publications/14\1120\memo\deferred\action.pdf.

[12] See Alfaro Garcia et al. v. Johnson et al., No. 14–cv–01775, slip op at 18 (N.D. Cal. Nov. 21, 2014) (denying Government's motion to dismiss and granting class certification).

[13] UNHCR, Unaccompanied Minors: Humanitarian Situation at U.S. Border http://www.unhcrwashington.org/children.

[14] See Complaint to the Department of Homeland Security, Office of Civil Rights and Civil Liberties and Inspector General, Re: Systemic Abuse of Unaccompanied Immigrant Children by U.S. Customs and Border Protection, June 11, http://immigrantjustice.org/sites/immigrantjustice.org/files/FINAL%20DHS%20Complaint%20re%20CBP%20Abuse%20of%20-UICs%202014%2006%2011.pdf.

[15] Id. at pp. 8–9.

[16] See Complaint to the Department of Homeland Security, Office of Civil Rights and Civil Liberties and Inspector General, Re: Inadequate U.S. Customs and Border Protection (CBP) screening practices block individuals fleeing persecution from access to the asylum process, Nov. 13, 2014, http://immigrantjustice.org/sites/immigrantjustice.org/files/FINAL%20DHS-%20Complaint%20re%20CBP%20Abuse%200f%20UICs%202014%2006%2011.pdf.

ing to the Status of Refugees (Refugee Convention) and the 1967 Protocol Relating to the Status of Refugees (Refugee Protocol), the United States is required to recognize as refugees anyone with a "well-founded fear" of persecution in their home countries, to accord refugees certain legal rights, and to refrain from returning them to countries where their safety would be threatened.[17] The United States ratified the Refugee Protocol[18] and in 1980, the United States enacted the Refugee Act to ensure compliance.[19] These obligations were also codified into the CBP Field Inspector's Manual. Despite this, NIJC and its partners across the country see many individuals who are either denied a chance to express fear of return or are ignored, and consequently sent back to places where their lives are threatened.

"R.S.C. is a woman from Guatemala who sought protection in the United States due to repeated persecution on account of her status as an indigenous woman. R.S.C. was harassed, abused, and raped on four occasions before fleeing her country for the first time in January 2014. She was deported twice from the United States and consequently suffered additional persecution in Guatemala. The first time she came to the United States, she tried to express her fear of return, but Border Patrol agents told her, 'Don't talk. These are all lies. Stop speaking . . . All Guatemalans are telling the same lies.' Upon her return to Guatemala, she was drugged, raped, and impregnated.[20] She returned to the United States in April 2014 seeking safety, and was again denied an opportunity to express her fear of return and was deported within days. She came to the United States for a third time with her 8-year-old son in July 2014, and they were placed in detention at the Artesia Family Residential Center in Artesia, New Mexico. Because CBP previously deported R.S.C., she is legally barred from applying for asylum and can only seek 'withholding of removal,' a much more limited form of protection with a higher burden of proof and no guarantee of permanency. Her son, however, is eligible to apply for asylum. As of the date of this writing, R.S.C. and her son remain detained while her removal proceedings are on-going."

R.S.C. is one of many who have been denied asylum protections due to inadequate screening by CBP Agents.[21] In addition to the nine complainants in NIJC's complaint, six legal service providers in Texas, California, and Arizona also provided statements showing that the complainants' experiences are not isolated incidents, but symptoms of systemic failures that result in permanent and life-threatening harm to hundreds—potentially thousands—of asylum seekers.

IV. RECOMMENDATIONS

Recent immigration from the Northern Triangle of Central America has been driven by violence and persecution and without addressing root causes in countries of origin, the trend that will likely continue. The increase in recent arrivals at the border may appear correlated in time with the availability of immigration relief for others with long-standing ties in the United States, but no causation between new arrivals and Executive Actions has been credibly established. Based on its experience and expertise, NIJC makes four recommendations that urge DHS to focus its attention on improvements at the border that promote due process and respect for the dignity of asylum seekers, including unaccompanied immigrant children:

(1) *End family detention.*—Because persecution is the main driver of migration for mothers and children from Central America, DHS should not use family detention as a deterrent nor signal that asylum seekers will be swiftly deported.

---

[17] "No Contracting State shall expel or return ('refouler') a refugee in any manner whatsoever to the frontiers of territories where his life or freedom would be threatened on account of his race, religion, nationality, membership of a particular social group or political opinion." Convention Relating to the Status of Refugees [hereinafter "Refugee Convention"], art. 33–1, 189 UNTS 150.

[18] Although the United States did not sign the Convention, the Protocol includes by reference the rights and duties set forth in the Convention. Refugee Protocol art. 2 ("The States Parties to the present Protocol undertake to apply Articles 2 to 34 inclusive of the Convention to Refugees as hereinafter defined.") The Protocol expanded these rights and duties to all refugees, whereas the Convention only applied to those displaced by the Second World War and its aftermath. Hereinafter, this statement cites to specific articles of the Convention when discussing the Protocol.

[19] *INS* v. *Cardoza-Fonseca,* 480 U.S. 421, 433 (1987) (citing the abundant evidence of an intent to conform the definition of "refugee" and our asylum law to the United Nation's Protocol to which the United States has been bound since 1968).

[20] Supra note 16 at page 18.

[21] Bekiempis, Victoria, "Is U.S. Customs and Border Protection Kicking Out Refugees?" *Newsweek,* Nov. 15, 2014, *http://www.newsweek.com/us-custom-sand-border-protection-kicking-out-refugees-284433.*

Families should receive individualized custody determinations, particularly once they have established a credible fear of persecution, and be considered for alternatives to detention, including bond, release on recognizance or orders of supervision, and community-based alternatives.

(2) Improve training of CBP Officers to ensure their understanding and compliance with existing law and procedure—including directives in the agency's own manual—with respect to the treatment of asylum seekers who are apprehended at the border or a point of entry.[22]

(3) *Promote clear information domestically and abroad on the parameters of recent Executive Action on immigration.*—Instead of seeking to deter asylum seekers from seeking safe haven in the United States, DHS should focus its effort on providing clear information through popular media in Spanish and indigenous languages, on the eligibility criteria for deferred action.

(4) *Ensure that children are treated fairly and humanely at the border.*—CBP must ensure that children are not held in their custody for more than 72 hours (and ideally not more than 24 hours) and promulgate binding short-term detention standards that apply to those held in CBP facilities.

STATEMENT OF THE AMERICAN IMMIGRATION LAWYERS ASSOCIATION

DECEMBER 2, 2014

The American Immigration Lawyers Association (AILA) is the National association of immigration lawyers established to promote justice, advocate for fair and reasonable immigration law and policy, advance the quality of immigration and nationality law and practice, and enhance the professional development of its members. AILA has over 13,000 attorney and law professor members.

On November 20, 2014, President Obama announced a package of reforms to the immigration system. AILA welcomes this plan which, for the most part, provides critically-needed changes to many aspects of our broken system. Almost 2 decades have passed since a major reform was enacted to the country's immigration laws, and despite efforts in recent years, Congress has been unable to complete the task. Though the Senate passed a comprehensive bill in 2013, the House has not yet passed any bills, including a border security bill that was passed by the Homeland Security Committee. In the absence of legislation, it would be irresponsible for the President to wait and do nothing while American families, businesses, and communities languish under the current system.

BORDER SECURITY

The President's announcement calls for additional border security measures at a time when the border has never been more secure. In the past decade, the Department of Homeland Security (DHS) has deployed unprecedented amounts of personnel, resources, and technology to secure the Nation's borders. Last year, in our report "Border Security: Moving Beyond Past Benchmarks," AILA urged lawmakers to stop the massive expenditure of resources on border security. AILA is disappointed that the President highlighted the plan in the 2013 Senate bill to add 20,000 more Border Patrol but offered no explanation for such an incredible increase. Until DHS provides justification for the need for such resources, this request for a dramatic increase in border personnel appears to be an unnecessary and wasteful expenditure of taxpayer resources.

AILA also opposes the planned surge in resources to the border that began this summer in response to the spike in families and unaccompanied children fleeing violence in the Northern Triangle in Central America. The surge included a massive expansion in family detention in gross violation of U.S. asylum and humanitarian law. It is undeniable that the violence in Guatemala, Honduras, and El Salvador has reached crisis proportions. Through AILA's volunteer project which provides legal representation for hundreds of families now detained in Artesia, NM, AILA has found that these families qualify for asylum at extremely high rates. Immigration judges have rendered decisions in 10 asylum cases where the mothers and children were represented by AILA attorneys, and in all 10 of those cases, the judges granted asylum. America is not confronted with a border security problem but a humanitarian crisis that affects the entire region. The crisis demands a humanitarian response not a deterrence-driven, border lockdown.

---

[22] See 8 U.S.C. § 1225(b)(1)(A)(ii); 8 CFR 235.3(b)(4); CBP Inspector's Field Manual, supra, note 36, at 113–14.

In the coming weeks and months, there will almost certainly be efforts to blame the continuing flow of unaccompanied minors and families fleeing violence in Central America on the President's two newly-announced deferred action programs (Deferred Action for Childhood Arrivals and Deferred Action for Parental Accountability). Such claims came during the summer despite the overwhelming evidence that what drove the surge in families and children to our country was the violence in those Central American countries. It is important to recognize that the United States has not seen large numbers of refugees from other extremely poor countries, such as Nicaragua, because Nicaragua has not experienced the same levels of uncontrollable violence.

Finally, the President's announcement, as of yet, includes nothing to address the grave and long-standing concerns about the lack of oversight and accountability of Border Patrol. Reports persist of Border Patrol abuses—including the excessive use of force resulting in civilian deaths at the border—deplorable detention conditions, racially-motivated arrests, coercive interrogation tactics, and the denial of access to asylum and the right to counsel. AILA recommends that the committee turn greater attention to these problems that are likely to grow more severe once DHS adds even more Border Patrol Agents to the Southern Border.

AMNESTY AND LEGAL AUTHORITY

The President's announcement has already engendered partisan debate and controversy. Many have alleged that his actions amount to a grant of amnesty. It is AILA's judgment that the President has acted well within his legal authority and that the deferred action programs do not constitute an amnesty. Unlike the 1986 amnesty President Reagan signed into law, deferred action does not confer formal legal status to the individual but merely a reprieve from immigration law enforcement, specifically deportation. Moreover the grant is temporary, so those granted the status could be at risk of deportation if the status expires. Finally, deferred action, by itself, does not provide a path to a green card or citizenship.

The Executive branch's authority to grant deferred action is derived from the Federal immigration statute and regulations as well as the long-standing principle of prosecutorial discretion used by every law enforcement agency. It is common practice for law enforcement agencies and their individual officers to decide how and to what extent to pursue a particular case based on established priorities. A law enforcement officer who declines to pursue a case against a person has favorably exercised prosecutorial discretion. In a 1999 letter, 28 Republican and Democratic Members of Congress (including the Chair of the Judiciary committee at that time, Lamar Smith) called for prosecutorial discretion in immigration enforcement: "The principle of the prosecutorial discretion is well-established."

Prosecutorial discretion ensures the smart use of finite enforcement resources. DHS cannot possibly deport everyone who is living unauthorized in the United States. Such a mass deportation is not only completely unrealistic but also an unwise policy choice as it would gravely fracture American society, negatively impact businesses, and hurt the economy. For these very reasons, Republican and Democratic leaders have spoken against the idea of deporting over 11 million undocumented immigrants. DHS and every other enforcement agency must choose priorities. Keeping America safe by focusing on those who present real threats to our National security and public safety is the right focus.

In the past 50 years, Republican and Democratic presidents have designated various groups of people for temporary relief from immigration enforcement by granting deferred action or using a similar tool. In 1990, President Bush provided blanket protection from deportation for up to 1.5 million unauthorized spouses and children of immigrants, about 40 percent of the total unauthorized population at the time. Other Presidents have provided temporary protection to victims of domestic violence, the family members of military service members, widows and widowers, as well as people from specific countries or regions such as Cuba, Haiti, Southeast Asia, or the Persian Gulf.

Deferred action is a vital tool that has been used historically to protect vulnerable populations. If DHS could not grant deferred action it would be unable to ensure that victims of domestic violence, sexual assault, human trafficking, and other crimes are protected from deportation while their applications for protections under the Violence Against Women Act (VAWA) are processed.

WHY IS IT NECESSARY FOR THE PRESIDENT TO ACT NOW?

In the absence of reform, the immigration system has become increasingly broken and is failing American families, businesses, and communities. Nation-wide polling has shown that Americans want major reform. A January 2014, Fox News poll

showed that 68 percent of Americans supported allowing illegal immigrants to remain the country and eventually qualify for citizenship if they meet certain requirements like paying taxes, learning English, and passing a background check. After
the November 2014 election, Edison Research, which does exit polling for the consor-
tium of major news networks, found that 57 percent of voters preferred that "illegal
immigrants working in the U.S." be offered legal status instead of deportation.

AILA hears daily from businesses that cannot hire workers and are stymied by
the slow and dysfunctional operations of the immigration system. Every day families
are kept separated because of long backlogs in the visa system. Now 11.5 million
people are living in the country without legal status. Most have families and jobs
but cannot work legally and must exist in the shadows. These individuals are also
subject to immigration enforcement and deportation. In the past several years, DHS
has deported hundreds of thousands of parents of U.S. citizens—approximately 23
percent of all deportations—causing painful separations of families.

America's immigration system is in urgent need of reform. AILA supports the en-
actment of legislation, the only way to provide lasting change. Until that happens
AILA applauds the efforts of the President and DHS to improve the system and implement reforms to the fullest extent permitted by law. AILA welcomes the opportunity to work with Congress and the President to make our system better for
America.

———

STATEMENT OF LAURA W. MURPHY, DIRECTOR, AND CHRISTOPHER RICKERD, POLICY
COUNSEL, ACLU WASHINGTON LEGISLATIVE OFFICE; VICKI B. GAUBECA, DIRECTOR,
AND BRIAN ERICKSON, POLICY ADVOCATE, THE ACLU OF NEW MEXICO, REGIONAL
CENTER FOR BORDER RIGHTS; CHRISTIAN RAMIREZ, DIRECTOR, SOUTHERN BORDER
COMMUNITIES COALITION; AND RYAN BATES, EXECUTIVE DIRECTOR, MICHIGAN
UNITED, RICH STOLZ, EXECUTIVE DIRECTOR, ONEAMERICA, AND STEVE CHOI, EXEC-
UTIVE DIRECTOR, NEW YORK IMMIGRATION COALITION, NORTHERN BORDERS COALI-
TION

DECEMBER 2, 2014

I. INTRODUCTION

For nearly 100 years, the American Civil Liberties Union (ACLU) has been our
Nation's guardian of liberty, working in courts, legislatures, and communities to defend and preserve the individual rights and liberties that the Constitution and the
laws of the United States guarantee everyone in this country. The ACLU takes up
the toughest civil liberties cases and issues to defend all people from Government
abuse and overreach. With more than a million members, activists, and supporters,
the ACLU is a Nation-wide organization that fights tirelessly in all 50 States, Puer-
to Rico, and Washington, DC, for the principle that every individual's rights must
be protected equally under the law, regardless of race, religion, gender, sexual ori-
entation, disability, or National origin. The ACLU's Washington Legislative Office
(WLO) conducts legislative and administrative advocacy to advance the organization's goal of protecting border residents' and immigrants' rights, including supporting a roadmap to citizenship for aspiring Americans.

The ACLU of New Mexico's Regional Center for Border Rights (RCBR) stands
with border communities to defend and protect America's Constitutional guarantees
of equality and justice for all families. The RCBR works in conjunction with ACLU
affiliates in California, Arizona, Texas, Michigan, Washington, and New York, as
well as advocates throughout the border region who comprise the Southern Border
Communities Coalition (SBCC) and the Northern Borders Coalition (NBC). SBCC
brings together more than 60 organizations from San Diego, California, to Brownsville, Texas, to ensure that border enforcement policies and practices are accountable and fair, respect human dignity and human rights, and prevent loss of life in
the region. NBC is a union of organizations along the Northern Border working to
stand up for civil and human rights together. The Coalition helps build shared strategies amongst members to address new border challenges, and collaborates with
partners in the Southwest to share best practices. The ACLU, SBCC, and NBC submit this statement to provide the committee with an appraisal of the civil liberties
implications of border security proposals.

The ACLU, SBCC, and NBC oppose exorbitant spending on border enforcement,
spending which is taking place without thoughtful consideration of current community and security needs. Current proposals to throw money, personnel, and equipment at the border would exacerbate the problems border communities face with
militarization today and ignore that:

- Deployment of additional border security resources along the U.S.-Mexico border would not be rooted in true border security needs. Over more than a decade, the U.S. Government has built a massive and comprehensive enforcement regime that has produced the most enforced border in U.S. history. Adding more resources would not only be wasteful and unnecessary, but would also be at odds with the top-of-the-charts safety, economic vitality, and diversity of border communities.
- Overall, border-wide apprehensions by U.S. Customs and Border Protection (CBP) are at their lowest levels in 40 years and net migration from Mexico at zero. This summer's migration of families and children fleeing violence in Central America and turning themselves in was correctly identified by CBP leadership as a humanitarian matter.
- Spending, with particular emphasis on the Southwest Border, has increased dramatically over the last decade with no commensurate accountability measures, resulting in civilian deaths at the hands of CBP personnel, unnecessary migrant deaths in the desert, and many other civil and human rights abuses on both our Nation's Southern and Northern Borders.

The U.S. Government cannot afford to throw money down the border-security drain, particularly because this spending has also damaged quality of life in border communities. The committee must not, without transparent and broad-ranging metrics, uncritically adopt the erroneous conventional wisdom of inadequate border security. Suggesting in a vacuum of information that more border enforcement resources are needed lacks fiscal responsibility and fails to give due attention to the true needs of border communities suffering from a wasteful, militarized enforcement regime. Moreover, justifying the additional deployment of border enforcement resources and family detention as an appropriate response to a humanitarian crisis in Central America contradicts our core values of compassion and justice for scared mothers and children.

The ACLU, SBCC, and NBC urge the committee to focus its efforts on ensuring that future border security is conducted humanely and in accordance with best police practices. Legislation should bring greater oversight and accountability—not war equipment or more boots on the ground—to CBP: Our Nation's largest law enforcement agency.

I. BORDER-SECURITY PROPOSALS MUST REJECT THE MISGUIDED, WASTEFUL APPROACH OF THE SENATE'S CORKER-HOEVEN "BORDER SURGE" AMENDMENT. INSTEAD, CONGRESS SHOULD END THE ABUSIVE MILITARIZATION OF BORDER COMMUNITIES.

a. The "Mini-Industrial Complex" of Border Spending

The committee has to this point, commendably, not followed the severely-misguided approach incorporated last year in Senate Bill 744's "surge" of border security resources. Such proposals ignore the fact that border security benchmarks of prior proposed or enacted legislation (in 2006, 2007, and 2010) have already been met or exceeded.[1] In the last decade, the United States has relied heavily on enforcement-only approaches to address migration, using deterrence-based border security strategies that have continued and expanded to record levels under the Obama administration:

- CBP has become an interior law enforcement agency through its vast claimed authority to patrol within 100 miles of all land and sea borders, an unnecessary overreach based on outdated regulations issued in the 1950s.
- Because of "zero-tolerance" initiatives like Operation Streamline, the Department of Homeland Security (DHS) now refers more cases for Federal prosecution than the Department of Justice's (DOJ) law enforcement agencies. Under President Obama, immigration-related Federal prosecutions have reached record levels at tremendous cost to U.S. taxpayers. Federal prisons are already more than 30 percent over capacity, due in large part to indiscriminate prosecution of individuals for crossing the border without authorization, often to rejoin their families.[2] The majority of those sentenced to Federal prison in 2013 were Latinos, who are now held in large numbers in substandard private prisons.[3]

[1] Chen, Greg and Kim, Su. "Border Security: Moving Beyond Past Benchmarks," AMERICAN IMMIGRATION LAWYERS ASSOCIATION, (Jan. 30, 2013), available at: http://www.aila.org/content/default.aspx?bc=25667143061.

[2] Carson, E. Ann. U.S. Department of Justice, BUREAU OF JUSTICE STATISTICS, "Prisoners in 2013" (Sept. 2014), available at: http://www.bjs.gov/content/pub/pdf/p13.pdf.

[3] U.S. Sentencing Commission, 2013 ANNUAL REPORT, Chapter 5, available at http://www.ussc.gov/sites/default/files/pdf/research-and-publications/annual-reports-and-sourcebooks/2013/2013\Annual\Report\Chap5\0.pdf; see also ACLU of Texas and ACLU, Warehoused and Forgotten: Immigrants Trapped in Our Shadow Private Prison System. (June

• Since 2003, the U.S. Border Patrol has doubled in size and now employs more than 21,400 agents, with about 85 percent of its force deployed at the U.S.-Mexico border. So many Border Patrol Agents now patrol the Southern Border that if they lined up equally from Brownsville to San Diego, they would stand in plain sight of one another. This number does not include the thousands of other DHS officials, including CBP Office of Field Operations officers and one-fourth of all Immigration and Customs Enforcement (ICE) personnel deployed at the same border. It also does not include 651 miles of fencing, 333 video surveillance systems, and at least 10 drones for air surveillance.

From a fiscal perspective, from fiscal year 2004 to fiscal year 2012, the budget for CBP increased by 94 percent to $11.65 billion, a leap of $5.65 billion; this following a 20 percent post-9/11 increase of $1 billion.[4] By way of comparison, this jump in funding more than quadrupled the growth rate of NASA's budget and was almost 10 times that of the National Institutes of Health. For fiscal year 2015, the administration's budget request for CBP was about $12.8 billion.[5] U.S. taxpayers now spend more on immigration enforcement agencies ($18 billion) than on the FBI, DEA, ATF, U.S. Marshals, and Secret Service—combined.

CBP's spending runs directly counter to data on recent and current migration trends and severely detracts from the true needs of border security. Much attention has been paid to increased apprehensions of children and families in south Texas, many of whom are fleeing terrible violence in Central America. When analyzed border-wide and over time, however, migrant apprehensions remain lower than at any time since the 1970s. Between 2000 and 2010, apprehensions by the Border Patrol declined more than 72 percent to about 463,000. In fiscal year 2013, Border Patrol apprehended almost 421,000 illegal crossers in total—fewer than in 2010 and an equivalent of less than two apprehensions a month per agent.[6]

The costs per apprehension vary per sector, but are generally at an all-time high. The Yuma, Arizona sector, for example, has seen a 95 percent decline in apprehensions since 2005 while the number of agents has tripled. Each agent was responsible for interdicting fewer than 7 immigrants in 2013, contributing to ballooning per capita costs: Each migrant apprehension at the border now costs five times more, rising from $1,400 in 2005 to over $7,500 in 2011.[7]

The Committee should heed House Appropriations Committee Chairman Hal Rogers' warning about the irrationality of border spending: "It is a sort of a mini industrial complex syndrome that has set in there. And we're going to have to guard against it every step of the way."[8] The committee's data-driven, bipartisan approach to border security, as embodied by H.R. 1417, the Border Security Results Act, is an improvement over proposals like the Corker-Hoeven "border surge." However, H.R. 1417's narrow focus on border security remains misplaced at a time when border enforcement is at an all-time high and continues to have a detrimental impact on border communities. It also sets flawed benchmarks in seeking a 90 percent "illegal crossing effectiveness rate" across the Southwest Border without contemplating a thorough study of border needs, particularly greater oversight and accountability and cross-border economic exchange.

b. Congress Must Expand Oversight and Accountability to Mitigate CBP Corruption and Abuse.

Unprecedented investment in border enforcement without corresponding oversight mechanisms has led to an increase in human and civil rights violations, traumatic family separations in border communities, and racial profiling and harassment of Native Americans, Latinos, and other people of color—many of them U.S. citizens and some who have lived in the region for generations. Corruption and criminal conduct have also plagued the dramatically and recklessly expanded CBP force, which,

2014), available at *https://www.aclu.org/sites/default/files/assets/060614-aclu-car-report-on-line.pdf.*

[4] Michele Mittelstadt et al., ''Through the Prism of National Security: Major Immigration Policy and Program Changes in the Decade since 9/11.'' (Migration Policy Institute, Aug. 2011), 3, available at *http://www.migrationpolicy.org/pubsFS23lPost-9-11policy.pdf.*

[5] Department of Homeland Security. ''Budget-in-Brief: Fiscal Year 2015,'' available at *http://www.dhs.gov/sites/default/files/publications/FY15BIB.pdf.*

[6] U.S Border Patrol, ''Nation-wide Illegal Alien Apprehensions Fiscal Years 1925–2013,'' available at: *http://www.cbp.gov/sites/default/files/documents/U.S.%20Border%20Patrol%20-Fiscal%20Year%20Apprehension%20Statistics%201925-2013.pdf.*

[7] Immigration Policy Center, Second Annual DHS Progress Report. (Apr. 2011), 26, available at *http://www.immigrationpolicy.org/sites/default/files/docs/2011lDHSlReportl041211.-pdf.*

[8] Ted Robbins, ''U.S. Grows An Industrial Complex Along The Border.'' NPR (Sept. 12, 2012), available at *http://www.npr.org/2012/09/12/160758471/u-s-grows-an-industrial-complex-along-the-border.*

as reported by *Politico Magazine,* had nearly one CBP Officer or Agent arrested for misconduct every single day from 2005 to 2012.[9] *Politico Magazine*'s exposé of CBP closely examines the now well-documented deficiencies in CBP's use-of-force policy and practice, which have led the agency to become one of our Nation's "deadliest" and most "out-of-control" law enforcement agencies. Since January 2010, at least 31 individuals have died from lethal force by CBP Officers and Agents. These cases include 14 individuals who were U.S. citizens and 6 individuals who were shot and killed while standing in Mexico—three of whom were teenagers, ages 15, 16, and 17.

In numerous cases individuals were shot multiple times, including through the back, such as Jose Antonio Elena Rodriguez who was struck by at least eight bullets—all but one in the back—across the border fence in Nogales, Sonora by agents responding to alleged rock throwing.[10] Also among the most well-known cases is that of Anastasio Hernandez Rojas who—by the happenstance of a witness video—was shown to be handcuffed and prostrate on the ground, contrary to the agency's incident reporting, when dozens of agents beat and Tased him to death. The San Diego coroner classified Mr. Hernandez's death as a homicide, noting in addition to a heart attack: "several loose teeth; bruising to his chest, stomach, hips, knees, back, lips, head and eyelids; five broken ribs; and a damaged spine." Both of these cases, and many more, illustrate common shortcomings in policy and practice that were criticized in an audit of CBP's use-of-force incidents conducted by the Police Executive Research Forum (PERF) and publicly released on May 30, 2014.

The *Arizona Republic* documented more than 46 deaths for which CBP is responsible since 2004–2005, and, as noted by the *Republic* in December 2013, in "none of [these] deaths has any agent or officer been publicly known to have faced consequences—not from the Border Patrol, not from Customs and Border Protection or Homeland Security, not from the Department of Justice, and not, ultimately, from criminal or civil courts."[11] Former head of CBP Internal Affairs James F. Tomsheck has flagged at least a quarter of 28 lethal force cases as "highly suspect," and alleged that "Border Patrol officials have consistently tried to change or distort facts to make fatal shootings by agents appear to be 'a good shoot' and cover up any wrongdoing." Perhaps most alarmingly of all, Tomsheck said he believes that thousands of employees hired by CBP during the agency's unprecedented expansion after 9/11 are potentially unfit to carry a badge and gun.[12] Lack of accountability for these unprofessional and dangerous personnel mars the reputations of officers and agents who conduct themselves properly.

CBP's failure to establish an institutional culture of accountability has far-reaching consequences for border communities, beyond excessive force. Numerous administrative complaints, legal claims, and reports documenting wide-spread CBP abuse in short-term custody facilities detail physical and verbal abuse, denial of medical care, failure to provide sufficient food and water, overcrowding, exposure to extreme temperatures, denial of communication with family and consular or legal support, failure to return personal belongings at the moment of repatriation, and use of coercion to pressure individuals into signing away legal rights. One New Mexican, Jane Doe, was held for hours by CBP officials who subjected her to repeated, invasive searches at a port of entry in El Paso, TX and subsequently a local hospital. After hours of humiliating searches she never consented to and which turned up no contraband, Ms. Doe was released with a hospital bill.[13]

CBP operates in an antiquated 100-mile zone extending toward the interior from any land or sea border, a distance that has no statutory basis and originated with-

[9] Graff, Garrett M. "The Green Monster: How the Border Patrol became America's most out-of-control law enforcement agency," POLITICO MAGAZINE (Nov./Dec. 2014), available at *http://www.politico.com/magazine/story/2014/10/border-patrol-the-green-monster-112220.-html#.VHdurlfF8Wk.*

[10] Skoloff, Brian. "Border Patrol Shot Mexican Teen Jose Antonio Elena Rodriguez 8 Times: Autopsy," ASSOCIATED PRESS (Feb. 8, 2013), available at *http://www.huffingtonpost.com/2013/02/08/border-patrol-shot-mexican-teen-jose-antonio-elena-rodriguez-autopsy\n\2646191.-html.*

[11] Crosby, Cherrill. "Change occurring after Republic's border investigation," ARIZONA RE-PUBLIC (Aug. 4, 2014), available at: *http://www.azcentral.com/story/news/politics/investigations/2014/08/02/border-force-republic-investigation-change/13534935/.*

[12] Becker, Andrew. "Removal of border agency's internal affairs chief raises alarms, "CENTER FOR INVESTIGATIVE REPORTING (June 12, 2014), available at: *http://cironline.org/reports/removal-border-agencys-internal-affairs-chief-raises-alarms-6443.*

[13] Planas, Roque. "Woman's Lawsuit Alleges Horrifying Abuse By Border Officers, Including Cavity Searches And Forced Bowel Movements," HUFFINGTON POST (Mar. 6, 2014), available at *http://www.huffingtonpost.com/2014/03/06/border-cavity-search\n\4907225.html.*

out scrutiny 60 years ago in now-outdated regulations.[14] The area includes two-thirds of the U.S. population, entire States like Florida and Maine, as well as almost all of the country's top metropolitan areas. This zone has converted CBP, particularly Border Patrol, into an interior enforcement agency that widely roams border communities.

By setting up interior checkpoints and conducting roving patrols many miles from the border, CBP does little to further border security goals but much to harm the quality of life of those who live and work in the border region. This includes communities like Arivaca, AZ, where residents have petitioned for the removal of one of three interior checkpoints that surround their community and have documented daily encounters between residents and agents. Their report found that Latino motorists were more than 26 times more likely to be asked to show identification, and 20 times more likely to be sent to secondary inspection.[15] But even non-Latino residents like Clarisa Christiansen and her children live in fear of the Border Patrol after agents pulled her over on a rural stretch of road near her house, threatened to cut her out of her seatbelt with a knife, and slashed her tires—all because she asked to know the reason agents stopped her.[16]

Northern Border residents have reported Border Patrol Agents conducting roving patrols near schools and churches and asking passengers for their documents on trains and buses that are traveling far from border crossings. The ACLU of Washington State brought and settled a class-action lawsuit to end the Border Patrol's practice of stopping vehicles and interrogating occupants without legal justification. One of the plaintiffs in the case was an African-American corrections officer and part-time police officer pulled over for no expressed reason and interrogated about his immigration status while wearing his corrections uniform.[17]

To expand border resources—particularly Border Patrol staffing—would badly worsen CBP's accountability crisis and compound the damage caused by prior hiring binges. It would also run contrary to the reality of border communities, which are safe,[18] diverse, and economically critical to this country. Our communities are forced to endure regular aggression, hostility, and intimidation from a significant percentage of CBP Officers and Agents. Border residents, like any community, should not have to live with fear and mistrust of law enforcement.

Border communities are a vital component of the half-trillion dollars in trade between the United States and Mexico, and the damaging effects of militarization on them must be addressed by serious oversight and accountability reforms to CBP. While the Federal Government has the authority to control our Nation's borders and regulate immigration, CBP officials must do so in compliance with National and international legal norms and standards.

As employees of the Nation's largest law enforcement agency, CBP officials should be trained and held to the highest law enforcement standards. Systemic, robust, and permanent oversight and accountability mechanisms for CBP must be the starting point for any discussion on border security:

- Equipping all CBP personnel with body-worn cameras;[19]
- Implementing enforceable custody standards;
- Reforming DHS complaint systems to provide a transparent, uniform process for filing complaints;[20] and

---

[4] See ACLU, The Constitution in the 100-Mile Border Zone (2014), available at *https://www.aclu.org/immigrants-rights/constitution-100-mile-border-zone.*

[15] Echevarri, Fernanda. Group Alleges Border Patrol is Racial Profiling at Arivaca Checkpoint, NATIONAL PUBLIC RADIO (Oct. 20, 2014), available at: *https://www.azpm.org/p/top-news/2014/10/20/47393-group-alleges-border-patrol-is-racial-profiling-at-arivaca-checkpoint/.*

[16] See video at ACLU website "Border Communities Under Siege," available at *https://www.aclu.org/border-communities-under-siege-border-patrol-agents-ride-roughshod-over-civil-rights.*

[17] Complaint available at *http://www.aclu-wa.org/sites/default/files/attachments/2012-04-26--Complaint10.pdf.*

[18] See, e.g., Frances Burns, "Rep. Cuellar: Texas cities on the Mexican border have less crime." UPI (Nov. 19, 2014) (quoting Congressman Cuellar: "Many people characterize the southern border as being unsafe but today's numbers paint a very different picture."), available at *http://www.upi.com/Top\News/US/2014/11/19/Rep-Cuellar-Texas-cities-on-the-Mexican-border-have-less-crime/3971416406308/.*

[19] See ACLU, "Strengthening CBP with the Use of Body-Worn Cameras." (June 27, 2014), available at *https://www.aclu.org/criminal-law-reform/strengthening-cbp-use-body-worn-cameras.*

[20] See ACLU et al., Recommendations to DHS to Improve Complaint Processing (2014), available at *https://www.aclu.org/sites/default/files/assets/14\5\5\recommendations\to\dhs\to\improve\complaint\processing\final.pdf;* see also American Immigration Council, *No Action Taken: Lack of CBP Accountability in Responding to Complaints of Abuse (2014),*

Continued

• Rolling back the antiquated 100-mile zone.

Such improvements would create a legacy of CBP reform that would improve the quality of life and restore trust for this and future generations of border residents.

CONCLUSION

Congress should transform border enforcement in a manner that is fiscally responsible, respects and listens to border residents before defining their communities' needs, and upholds Constitutional rights and American values. The ACLU, SBCC, and NBC commend the House Committee on Homeland Security for its past commitments to define border security with precision before funneling more resources. We urge the committee to prioritize reduction of CBP abuses in the currently-oppressive border and immigration enforcement system which has cost more than $250 billion in today's dollars since 1986.[21]

Chairman McCAUL. I want to remind the Members of this committee that the Secretary has 30 minutes left, so if you can keep your remarks as short as possible.

With that, Mr. Vela.

Mr. VELA. Mr. Secretary, if I had known we could have played clips, I was reminded of a scene from Cheech and Chong with the background music of coming to America. If anybody had an interest they can probably find it on YouTube. But I, too, want to thank you for your accessibility since having taken office, and I just want to say that since we have been dealing with you and your staff we have seen marked changes and progress between communications between this committee and yours.

I think with respect to the idea of border security, you were asked about metrics, the fact is, is that this committee in a fully bipartisan fashion almost a year ago passed a border security bill that would have established those metrics, and we have yet to see it on the House floor. We have 2 weeks left before the end of the year. If that bill was brought to the House floor, you would have a border security bill by the end of the year.

With respect to the issue of a permanent solution in the context of immigration, the fact of the matter is, is our choices are very stark in my view. There are those who believe that of the millions of people who have been working here in our construction sites, our hotels, our restaurants, and all across this country, that what we ought to do is rope them up and send them back. There are those who believe that we ought to develop a pathway to citizenship and a legalization process. What I strongly object to—and remember that I agree we need border security. That is why I voted on the bill that passed this committee—what I strongly object to is the idea that the legalization process ought to be conditioned on border security, because to me if you define border security as making sure that we prevent people from coming here in the future, I don't see what that has to do with the people that are already here.

I also cringe when I hear the word border crisis because in my view what we are talking about is three separate crises that are interrelated. That is the crisis of drug smuggling, human smuggling, and illegal migration. The fact is, is that those are crises that do not end or begin at the border. They begin with economic conditions in Mexico and Central America and issues of cartel violence in Central America and Mexico as well, and they end with our de-

available at *http://www.immigrationpolicy.org/special-reports/no-action-taken-lack-cbp-account-ability-responding-complaints-abuse*.
[21] Robbins, supra.

mand for drugs on this side of the border as well as the fact when you consider the fact that over a thousand cities across this country, FBI statistics shows that there is a cartel presence.

So I really believe that if we are ever going to really address the root causes of those three issues, that we really have to start talking about issues of economic development in Mexico and Central America and addressing cartel violence. With that in mind, what I would ask, and this may be coming from left field because I know it is more of a Department of Justice matter, in the last year the former governor of Tamaulipas, Mexico, was indicted in the Southern District of Texas and an extradition order has been issued by the Federal judge down in Brownsville, and I would just ask that you do whatever you can with respect to the other department heads to see if we cannot bring this gentleman to justice. Because when we talk about drug smuggling, we talk about human smuggling, the fact of the matter is, it is not the coyotes making the money, it is the people at the top.

I yield the rest of my time.

Secretary JOHNSON. Congressman, may I respond?

Chairman MCCAUL. Yes, sir.

Secretary JOHNSON. Just briefly. I have this thought listening to you, Congressman. Negotiating and arriving at an acceptable piece of legislation that addresses our immigration system in a comprehensive way, in my judgment, should not be that hard. I have in my private law practice negotiated the most complex civil settlements ever on Wall Street. I believe that if we could just strip away the emotion and the politics on this issue and you brought me the right group of Members of the House of Representatives, I could negotiate a bill with you, and I am issuing that invitation again. I believe we could do it. It should not be that difficult.

Chairman MCCAUL. Thank you.

The Chairman now recognizes Mr. Barletta.

Mr. BARLETTA. Thank you, Mr. Chairman.

Mr. Secretary, some people say that our economic security is National security. Nearly 20 million Americans woke up this morning either unemployed or underemployed. Now, the President didn't mention these Americas when he announced his plan to grant de facto amnesty and work permits to up to 5 million illegal immigrants. He didn't discuss the competition this would create for them or the impact it would have on their pocketbooks. Your series of memoranda outlining this policy for him didn't mention them either.

To address this problem and protect the American worker, I introduced legislation prior to the President's announcement that would make clear that illegal immigrants benefiting from his Executive amnesty are not authorized to work in the United States. When it comes to illegal immigration, the conversation is always about the illegal immigrant, not about the people that it will affect. You see, Mr. Secretary, I don't think it is fair, especially around the holidays, to put illegal immigrants ahead of the American worker.

Secretary Johnson, the President keeps saying that his Executive Action will boost the economy. So tell me, how will adding at least

5 million new competitors to the workforce make it easier for the unemployed Americans to find a job?

Secretary JOHNSON. Congressman, the fact is, as I am sure you know, that we have lots of undocumented in this country working off the books. If that is not apparent, then I suggest you spend some time in a restaurant here in the Washington, DC, area to see it for yourself. What we want to do is encourage those people to get on the books, and I will provide them a work authorization so that they may legally continue in the employment they now have.

Mr. BARLETTA. But how does that make it easier for the American worker? We keep talking about the illegal immigrant. Here we go again talking about the illegal immigrant and how we can make it easier for them. How does this help the American worker who can't find work and can't provide for his family? Who is fighting for them? Why don't we talk about the American worker and what this will do to them, not what it will do for the illegal immigrant?

Secretary JOHNSON. Well, the economy is getting better, as I am sure you know. The question of U.S. jobs, American jobs, is in my view a separate issue. What I want to do——

Mr. BARLETTA. So adding 5 million more competitors for these jobs will make it easier?

Secretary JOHNSON. If I may finish my sentence. The estimate is that the potential class is up to 4 million. Not all of those will apply. The goal is to encourage these people who are now working off the books, and we do have undocumented immigrants in this country working off the books, to get on the books, pay taxes into the Federal Treasury pursuant to a work authorization. The assessment is that that will not impinge upon American jobs with American workers.

Mr. BARLETTA. Mr. Secretary, is it true that the illegal immigrants who were granted amnesty will not need to comply with the Affordable Care Act?

Secretary JOHNSON. Those who are candidates for and are accepted into the deferred action program will not be eligible for comprehensive health care, ACA.

Mr. BARLETTA. So therefore an employer may have a decision to make: Do I keep the American worker and provide health insurance or pay a $3,000 fine or do I get rid of the American worker and hire someone who I do not have to provide health insurance and I won't get fined? Is that a possibility?

Secretary JOHNSON. I don't see it that way.

Mr. BARLETTA. You don't think any employers will see it that way?

Secretary JOHNSON. I don't think I see it that way, no. No, sir.

Mr. BARLETTA. Following the 9/11 Commission report, the Commission staff issued a report on terrorist travel that made connections between enforcement of our immigration laws and National security. On Page 98 of that report it describes how terrorists would benefit from any form of amnesty. The report recognized that terrorists in the 1990s, as well as the September 11 hijackers, needed to find a way to stay in or embed themselves in the United States if their operational plans were to come to fruition. This tells us what we all know, that terrorists want two things. They want to get into this country, and then they want to stay here.

Mr. Secretary, does the President's Executive Action facilitate just that by not heeding the advice of the 9/11 Commission and its staff, and how can this administration justify its Executive Actions on immigration when it directly contradicts their findings?

Secretary JOHNSON. The reality is that we have an estimated 11.3 million undocumented in this country. From my Homeland Security perspective and from the perspective of someone whose principal mission is counterterrorism, I want to see those people come out of the shadows. I want to encourage people——

Mr. BARLETTA. But you did testify in the last hearing——

Secretary JOHNSON. If I may finish my sentence. I want people to submit to criminal background checks and come out of the shadows. The problem we have right now is we have 11 million people in this country and we do not know who they are from the perspective of what you just read from that 9/11 Commission report. We are vulnerable. I want people to come out of the shadows——

Mr. BARLETTA. Mr. Secretary, you testified at the last hearing, and you agreed with me and your words were, most criminals do not subject themselves to criminal background checks.

Secretary JOHNSON. I want as many as possible to submit to criminal background checks.

Mr. BARLETTA. Thank you, Mr. Chairman.

Chairman McCAUL. Let me just say to the remaining Members, due to the time constraints of the Secretary, we are going to limit questioning to 3 minutes by unanimous consent. Without objection, so ordered.

The Chairman now recognizes Mr. Swalwell from California.

Mr. SWALWELL. Mr. Secretary, does the number 2,577,516 mean anything to you?

Secretary JOHNSON. It sounds familiar. I am not sure why it sounds familiar.

Mr. SWALWELL. Would it surprise you to learn that according to the American Immigration Council this is the number of immigrants granted temporary relief by Republican Presidents over the last 50 years?

Secretary JOHNSON. That is news to me. That is a big number.

Mr. SWALWELL. Would it surprise you that not a single person who has sat on this dais with me, particularly among my GOP colleagues, made a single public statement criticizing any Executive Actions taken by any Republican Presidents with respect to immigration?

Secretary JOHNSON. I am not sure what to say.

Mr. SWALWELL. Our Chairman has brought up a number of times that we have a bipartisan bill, something that I admire, that he was able to shepherd through this committee, yet it has not come to the floor for a vote. It is frustrating to me that we are bringing you here to criticize the President's actions, yet Speaker Boehner has a bill that addresses border security that has not been brought to the floor. I believe that in many ways, by silencing both sides of this issue by not allowing a vote, the Speaker in many ways is taking his own Executive Action that refuses to allow people who oppose immigration reform and those who support it to even be a voice of their district and take a vote.

So with that in mind, I want to know, among the 11.3 million undocumented immigrants, do you know, Mr. Secretary, how prioritizing felons over families for deportation, what that will do to make us safer as opposed to what we have been doing prior?

Secretary JOHNSON. Well, the guidance that I issued is guidance in clearer terms that spells out exactly the types of offenses that are priority 1s, priority 2s. When we did our review, we found that there was a fair amount of ambiguity in the existing guidance that needed to be cleaned up because there was a lot of misunderstanding in the field that led to some of the cases of heartache that we all hear about. So the guidance is clearer.

With that is a restart of the Secure Communities Program. Secure Communities is intended to get at criminals who are undocumented in jail. But there is a lot of resistance now to Secure Communities. So an integral part of this promoting public safety is a fresh start on the Secure Communities Program.

The last thing I will say is when we talk about a bill, I believe the Speaker's desire for comprehensive immigration reform is genuine. I will say again that I am interested in working with Members of this committee, Members of the House of Representatives on a piece of legislation or pieces of legislation that addresses our system in a comprehensive way, in a way that our Executive Actions cannot reach.

Mr. KING [presiding]. The time of the gentleman has expired.

The gentleman from Florida, Mr. Clawson.

Mr. CLAWSON. Thank you for coming today, Mr. Secretary. I am not going to harangue you or badger you, and I will ask you to be quick with me so we can get right to what I want to know in all sincerity.

In previous meetings that I have been here, I have been told a little bit of what you have said today, which we need more resources. Eight billion dollars is the backlog of CapEx for ports and so forth, as I understand. Going to spend $800 million on new ports in the next 5 years, some of your border folks have told us. But when we ask for operational data to know what the bang for the buck is for the taxpayer, we really get very little data. If I was a board member and you and I were back in our previous lives, I would say, how can I say okay to more resources and more effort, more taxpayer involvement, when I don't know the return on investment for the CapEx and I don't know what the operational effectiveness is other than really macro data? Can you shed any light on that? Am I missing the boat here?

Secretary JOHNSON. Well, I will shed light on my commitment to more transparency. I think part of the problem we have is lack of coherent data. So one of the things I directed in the Executive Actions that we issued week before last is I directed the Office of Immigration Statistics to create the capacity to collect, maintain, and report to the Secretary data reflecting the numbers of those apprehended, removed, returned, or otherwise repatriated, by any component of DHS. I also intend that this data be part of a package of data released by DHS to the public annually.

So I am sympathetic to what you are saying, and I would like to see us in addition to this develop metrics for how we define border security so that the Congress and the public understands what we are driving for.

Mr. CLAWSON. But I just don't know how much bang for the buck we are getting for the taxpayer dollar. So in addition to how many people we are capturing and how many are getting through, what is the return on investment for the money we are spending? It is hard for me to say yes or no to what is being asked if I don't know how well we are spending the current money and the money that has been——

Secretary JOHNSON. I would encourage you, if you haven't already, to look at the speech I gave on border security in October to a think tank called CSIS, where I laid out a lot of the investment and a lot of the data concerning apprehensions of illegal immigrants to get at a clearer picture of what you are getting on the return on your investment.

Mr. CLAWSON. Any data that would help us understand how well the Department is working will make it easier for us to be open-minded to working together as you say. Thank you.

Secretary JOHNSON. There is a misapprehension that things are as worse as they have ever been. In fact, apprehensions of illegal immigrants is a fraction of what it used to be, in large part because of the investment that this Congress has made in border security we are seeing a return on investment. I think we can do better, but we have invested a lot in surveillance, personnel, as the Chairman knows and others, over the last 15 years, and we have seen a return on investment. Apprehensions used to be 1.6 million. They are now down to between 400,000 and 500,000. But I believe we can do better.

Mr. KING. The time of the gentleman has expired.

The gentlelady from California is recognized.

Ms. SANCHEZ. Thank you, Mr. Chairman.

Thank you, Secretary, for being before us. I had the pleasure of working with you when you were over at the Defense Department, and I am glad you are staying on at Homeland because this is a very, very critical time. I am worried, being double-hatted sitting on Defense and Homeland, I am worried about threats from ISIS and terrorists and coming into our country or being embedded in our country or some would say mentoring candidate or what have you, but here we are. We are here to protect America and to protect Americans. So thank you for the work that you and all the people who work in your Department do on our behalf.

I want to go back to something that you said, the whole issue of having background checks on people, because I live in California. We have a lot of people there who for whatever reason don't have the right documents to be in our country. Some actually would qualify and have qualified under our programs, under the legal, but if they have to wait 10 years away from a loved one because they have to wait outside of the country, they have probably broken that and they have decided to stay and live those 10 years here with their loved one or their child rather than do what we do to them, which is to push them out for 10 years. There are people who just—it has taken too long. The backlog is just so long for some of these people to get through the process even though they qualify under everything.

So I am thrilled that we are going to get good people who are our deacons in our churches, they are PTA moms, to come forward, to give us their data, to give us their fingerprints, to pay a fine, and to say, let us work, let us go on with our lives here, especially if they have USA-born children or legal residents. I am thrilled that the President understands that.

But I am even more thrilled about it because that allows these limited resources that we have to be trained on the people that I really want to go after, and that is these terrorists and these threats to our country. A lot of people say, well, you are Hispanic, Loretta, so you care about the Latino community. I have to tell you, I have got one of the largest Asian populations in the Nation. I have got Romanians. I have got all sorts of people who have come from other countries, many of them working, some of them paying taxes, but many of them working and wanting to get on an even footing here in the United States.

So I just want to thank you, Mr. Secretary, because I know that you sat down and you took a look and you used your lawyer skills and everybody else's skills to sit down and figure out how do we make sure that the limited resources we have are trained on the bad guys, not on the people who are really part of our American family? So I just want to thank you.

Mr. KING. Time of the gentlelady has expired.

Gentleman from South Carolina.

Mr. SANFORD. Thank you, Mr. Chairman.

Mr. Secretary, delighted to be with you again. I have but 3 minutes, I am going to try and ask three quick questions, and therefore I would ask for your brevity if possible.

First question is, I mean, fundamentally a question about fairness, which is I think one of the things that a lot of people struggle with on the notion of the President's Executive and unilateral action is that it will put a lot of families from around the world in essence in a second-class bus. My question to you would be: Is it fair to those families who have been waiting in the queue in terms of immigration to go behind a bunch of folks that in essence will get favorable status based on the Executive Action?

Secretary JOHNSON. Well, that is not what we have done, sir. Through Executive Action we cannot grant citizenship, we cannot put somebody in the head of the line for citizenship, and we are not granting lawful permanent residence. Deferred action is simply for a period of time a determination that someone should be lawfully present in the country, which is a significantly lower form of status.

Mr. SANFORD. Fair enough, but it is de facto citizenship in that they are able to live here, work here, raise families here, et cetera. I will quickly move on to the second question.

Secretary JOHNSON. In fact, they already are.

Mr. SANFORD. What is that?

Secretary JOHNSON. In fact they already are.

Mr. SANFORD. They are, but they don't have the legal claim to our entitlement system that they now will. I mean, if you look at our entitlement system, it is $18 trillion in the hole, and most of them are based on being lawfully present in this country to be eligible for entitlements. So, I mean, how do you say to that family in Mississippi who has been struggling to make it, our entitlement system is based in paying for the whole of your life, you get to the retirement age, and then you begin to collect, what do you say to that family, your retirement system, your health care system as it is provided by Government will be less financially solvent than it would have been based on this unilateral action? What would you say in terms of fairness there?

Secretary JOHNSON. I would say that the people we are talking about are already here. They have been here for years. They have become integrated members of society, and I want them to come forward——

Mr. SANFORD. But they are not going to collect Social Security or Medicare——

Secretary JOHNSON [continuing]. And contribute to the tax base of this country.

Mr. SANFORD. But they won't collect the way they will, and the question is: Do you get more than you give? The *Wall Street Journal* had a very interesting editorial within the last 2 weeks on that very point. I see I am down to 34 seconds.

The last question is, in your opening statements, a lot of the attributes that you defined could be handled perfectly by work permits. Why not just do work permits rather than this de facto sort of quasi-citizenship that comes with this Executive Action?

Secretary JOHNSON. Work authorization is something the Secretary of Homeland Security has the authority to give by statute to someone who has been granted deferred action, so that is what we did.

Mr. SANFORD. I see I have 3 seconds, Mr. Chairman. I would go for a second question, but don't have it.

Mr. KING. You guys speak more slowly than we do.

The gentlelady from New York, Ms. Clarke.

Ms. CLARKE. Thank you, Mr. Chairman.

There was a statement made earlier by the gentleman from South Carolina, Mr. Duncan, that I know was a gross generalization about the American people as it relates to the Executive Order issued by President Obama. So for the record, overwhelmingly the Americans in my district laud and support what President Obama has done, and they have your back.

I want to ask Secretary Johnson, the President's Executive Action was certainly a step in the right direction, and for many it speaks to the moral, social, and family-related reasons that will have a positive effect on our civil society.

However, I want to get to the economics of this, because it has been raised by a number of colleagues and particularly Mr. Barletta. It was estimated recently by the Center for American Progress that this Executive Action will raise an additional $3 billion in payroll taxes in the first year alone, and $22.6 billion over 5 years as workers and employers get on the books and begin paying taxes for the first time. Even individual States will gain from this. Do you believe that the economic factors like these should play a role in determining our immigration policy?

Second, the issue of Securing the Cities. The program fingerprints individuals booked in State and local jails and submitted electronically to the FBI for criminal background checks. It allows

ICE to identify potentially removable individuals. The question is, the program has been controversial, both legally and politically, as you know. It is my understanding that the Priority Enforcement Program, which will replace Securing the Cities under the administration's plan, will rely on the same technology as Securing the Cities but would focus on individuals in State and local custody who have been convicted of felonies and significant misdemeanors. Please explain how PEP will maintain the biometrics collection and background checks under Securing the Cities while also addressing important concerns raised by the courts, advocates, and local communities about Securing the Cities.

Secretary JOHNSON. Well, you characterized it accurately. To address the legal concerns that are arising in litigation we are no longer going to be putting detainers on people. Instead we will have request for notification. A detainer in litigation has often, and the court determines that State and local law enforcement did not have the legal authority to hold that person simply because of a detainer when they would have otherwise released them. So in place of that, we are going to have request for notification so that we are notified before the individual is released, unless we have probable cause to tell the NYPD, for example, that the person is undocumented and will be removed.

I agree with your question about, should economics play a role in immigration policy? I am not an economist. I will refer you to the President's Council of Economic Advisors' analysis which was issued week before last on the impact of our Executive Actions on the economy.

Ms. CLARKE. Thank you.

Mr. KING. The time of the gentlelady has expired, and I now recognize myself for the purpose of questioning.

Secretary, it is good to see you today. Thank you for being here.

Let me begin my questioning on a positive note. I was in a meeting the other night with a number of Republicans from New York who strongly opposed the Executive Order, but several of them went out of their way to say they had dealt with you as a lawyer and they have the highest regard for your integrity and professionalism. Totally unsolicited, they made a point of saying that first. I agreed with them.

Secretary JOHNSON. It goes downhill from here. Thank you.

Mr. KING. Downhill, yeah.

No, I am opposed to the Executive Order for a number of reasons. We can discuss, you know, the legal merits of it, but I am influenced greatly by the *Youngstown Sheet and Tube* case, where Justice Jackson—where the Court struck down the Executive Action by President Truman, and he was saying that Executive Action in questionable cases must be scrutinized with caution. Because he said, what is at stake is the equilibrium established by a Constitutional system.

That is what I see here as being—apart from all the legalities, which I think are significant, is the fact that, for the American people to have faith in the Government, they should feel that there is good faith coming from both sides.

In this case, we had the President time and again saying he did not have the power to do this. We have the fact that any time over the last 6 years the President could have issued this Executive Order, the fact that he did not issue the Executive Order until after the elections were over.

If the President felt there was a consensus among the American people, then this should have been part of the campaign debates. That is how in a democracy people express their views. The fact is, they were virtually silent on this issue throughout the campaign. The campaign is over, Republicans win both houses, and then the President issues this order.

I would say that if the President is sincere about wanting legislation and if he believes he has the right to issue this order, why didn't he say he realizes things have changed in the Congress, he disagrees with the fact that the House did or did not act, and set a deadline of July 1, and as of July 1 he could issue his Executive Order, we could take what action we want against it, whether it is legislative, whether it is appropriations-wise?

But during that 6 months, the President would have an opportunity to frame the National debate on trying to come to an immigration bill. He would be able to focus attention on it. Then you would have seen Republicans in the House and the Senate being in a position where they would have to deal with the President.

Then if July 1 comes along and there is no—I am using that as an arbitrary date; it could be any date—then the President could issue the Executive Order, and the American people could decide who was right and who was wrong. Congress could take what action it felt it had to. The President, through you, could go ahead and implement the order.

So I just feel—and I use these words advisedly—that there was bad faith in issuing the Executive Order at this time. If we are trying to get the confidence of the American people, this is not the way to do it.

Secretary JOHNSON. I guess, in response, Chairman, I would say we did do that. We did exactly that. We said we were going to do this in the spring, and the President decided to wait over the summer to see whether the Congress would act.

The Speaker, whose desire for immigration reform I believe is genuine, had hoped that he could get immigration reform through the House of Representatives. That did not happen. The President said he would wait. The Speaker told him, we are not going to get a bill.

Then we decided to wait until after the mid-terms, even further, and here we are. We have done a lot of waiting. We waited for several years, sir.

Mr. KING. I just think the President's Executive Order—again, the impression it would leave is he is trying to undo the impact of the election. If he felt that strongly about it, he should have issued it before the campaign.

But my time has expired, and I am not trying to end your discussion. Again, my respect for you.

Now my friend from New Jersey, Mr. Payne.

Mr. PAYNE. Thank you, Mr. Chairman.

Mr. Secretary, always a pleasure to see you here. I want to say that I am also delighted that you will be staying on at Homeland Security. I think that you, in your time there, have brought that organization together tighter and more efficient. For that, I thank you.

It is my understanding that this Executive Order—this Executive Action will only last for 2 years under the Obama administration, and it is not clear what will happen to the millions who are affected under DACA and now DAPA when the administration is over. This creates a lot of uncertainty, in my opinion, and underscores the need for Congressional action to clear up and fix this broken immigration system.

So, in your opinion, what will happen to the children and parents who are being encouraged now to come out of the shadows in 2 years if nothing happens?

Secretary JOHNSON. Well, the nature of Executive Action is that the next Executive can undo it. I would hope that that would not happen here. Administration to administration, we do not typically undo administrative Actions, Executive Orders, particularly where you are affecting in what I think would be a rather harsh manner the lives of people who are here in this country.

So my hope is, first, over the next 2 years, there is legislation that, in effect, addresses the same phenomenon in the same way. But in the absence of that, my hope is that these Executive Actions are sustained as good Government policy.

Going forward—I want to emphasize this—going forward, those apprehended who came here illegally January 1, 2014, under our existing policy, are priorities for removal and will not be eligible for deferred action going forward. So there is a clear demarcation between those who have been here for years and those who would think to come here in the future illegally. Those people will be priorities.

Mr. PAYNE. How can Congress help ensure that these millions of people are not encouraged to go back into the shadows in 2 years?

Secretary JOHNSON. Support us through legislation.

Mr. PAYNE. So it is really time Congress stood up and helped fix this problem rather than throwing darts at the administration.

Secretary JOHNSON. That is my hope. I believe that it is a solvable problem legislatively, and I believe that if we can remove the emotion and the politics we can achieve it. There are several Members of this committee who I believe I could work with on a comprehensive solution legislatively.

Mr. PAYNE. Thank you, Mr. Secretary.

I yield back.

Chairman MCCAUL [presiding]. The Chairman recognizes Mr. Meehan.

Mr. MEEHAN. Thank you, Mr. Chairman.

Thank you, Secretary, for being here. You know I have a great deal of respect for you. You are an attorney. But I have some fundamental disagreements with a couple of the points that were made, and I just need your articulation on this.

You are the one who said somehow somebody may be—what you are doing is creating an opportunity for them to lawfully be here in the country. Now, I think it is an unquestioned point that, as the law stands today, anybody who illegally enters the United States is a deportable alien. That is the Congressional intent.

But what has happened by this directive is the President has stepped into the authority of Congress, the Constitutional authority, to determine that, under the existing law, you have identified that somebody will lawfully be here so long as they—using prosecutorial discretion, they won't be deported if they are not a threat to National security, aren't a threat to public safety, or aren't a threat to border security.

How can you create a class of people who are beyond prosecution and not be violating the Constitutional separation of powers in which Congress has clearly articulated its intent?

Secretary JOHNSON. Well, first, during the period of deferred action—that is what it is, deferred action—you can lose membership in that program if you commit a crime, for example.

Mr. MEEHAN. But you can also have a lawfully articulated ability under the President's directive to be here if you don't. That is an expression of a Constitutional protection that does not exist except for the President's overreach of prosecutorial discretion.

Secretary JOHNSON. Congressman, this type of action has existed in one form or another going back decades. It was exercised in the Reagan and Bush administrations——

Mr. MEEHAN. No, Mr. Secretary, I will not allow you to go there. It was exercised after authorized activity by the Congress in which they were continuing to——

Secretary JOHNSON. To protect a class of people that the Congress did not.

Mr. MEEHAN. No, but the Congress already clearly articulated an intent to include those, and there was the fulfilling of Congressional intent. Here, you have created a class of people in contravention of Congressional intent.

Secretary JOHNSON. Well, first of all, an assessment of deferred action will be made on a case-by-case basis.

Now, if I may, sir, the way I look at it is this. I know you will appreciate this. When I was an assistant United States attorney, we used to—and I am sure this was true in your office when you were a U.S. attorney—we used to enter into deferred prosecution agreements with individuals. You committed a crime, or you may have committed a crime, you have been charged, but if you, in effect, behave for the next 6 months, 12 months, a year, whatever, we are going to defer prosecution——

Mr. MEEHAN. I understand that. My time is limited.

Secretary JOHNSON. That is, in effect, what we are doing here.

Mr. MEEHAN. We all understand prosecutorial discretion. This changes that, however, which creates a class of people, despite prosecutorial discretion, who may be here because the President created that category, not Congress. That is a clear violation of the Constitutional principles. Apart from our desire to work together, he is acting in a capacity beyond where he has the ability to do so.

Secretary JOHNSON. Sir, I respectfully disagree.

Mr. MEEHAN. On what basis?

Secretary JOHNSON. They are present—they are lawfully present in this——

Mr. MEEHAN. Lawfully? How are they lawfully here when the intention of Congress was very clear, they can be deportable? It doesn't mean they will be deportable——

Secretary JOHNSON. But, sir——

Mr. MEEHAN [continuing]. But now you are saying——

Secretary JOHNSON [continuing]. The Congress has not given me the resources to deport 11 million people.

Mr. MEEHAN. I appreciate that fact.

Secretary JOHNSON. That does not exist. They are here.

Mr. MEEHAN. That is prosecutorial discretion——

Secretary JOHNSON. So, if I may——

Mr. MEEHAN [continuing]. If they are not lawfully here.

Secretary JOHNSON. If I may——

Mr. MEEHAN. We are choosing—every speeder on 95 could be stopped, but we can't stop everyone, but that doesn't mean that they aren't going over the speed limit. Your level says there is no speed limit.

Secretary JOHNSON. If I may finish my sentence. They are here. From my Homeland Security perspective, I want them to come forward and get on the books and receive a work authorization——

Mr. MEEHAN. Mr. Secretary, they are here, but you said they were lawfully here. Under Congressional intent, they are not lawfully here. Yet the President has created that category out of whole cloth.

Secretary JOHNSON. This is a form of Executive Action that was not invented in this administration. It goes back decades, sir.

Mr. MEEHAN. Secretary, it was. I am sorry to disagree with you.

Chairman MCCAUL. The gentleman's time has expired.

Mr. MEEHAN. I will work with you, but I disagree with you.

Chairman MCCAUL. Mr. Perry from Pennsylvania.

Mr. PERRY. Thank you, Mr. Chairman.

Mr. Secretary, appreciate your service.

Is there a forged document system present that has been operating for some time that allows illegal immigrants to avoid the law?

Secretary JOHNSON. I am sorry. What was your question?

Mr. PERRY. Is there a forged document system present in some form around the border, where people that would come here illegally obtain Social Security numbers and other documents that provide them access to America to——

Secretary JOHNSON. In other words, a criminal network that provides false——

Mr. PERRY. Whatever you want to call it. Is there one present?

Secretary JOHNSON. I would imagine that there is, sir.

Mr. PERRY. Is using forged documents to gain access to the Nation, employment, social services, et cetera, would we consider that lawful?

Secretary JOHNSON. I do not believe so, no.

Mr. PERRY. Okay. I would agree with you.

What is the DHS estimate for those here illegally, including those with terrorist affiliations or motives, who have used falsified documentation to gain access to our Nation and the other things I described?

Secretary JOHNSON. I don't have that number off-hand, but I can get it for you.

Mr. PERRY. You have a number?

Secretary JOHNSON. Well, if there is such an estimate, I will undertake to get it to you.

Mr. PERRY. Okay. Listen, I am sure there is an estimate. I am sure it is just an estimate, because they are unlawful. But I will also say that we have written your office on several occasions requesting information and have not gotten any answers. So I am just concerned about the ability or your willingness to give us those answers.

But let me just cite a couple examples for you.

We have Major League Baseball players who have become MVPs, made millions of dollars, and after the fact we found out as Americans that they weren't here lawfully and used forged documents. These are very high-profile people.

An individual in California, deported three times, came back on the fourth time and shot a police officer dead.

You have an individual that was residing in North Carolina, came up to Baltimore, kidnapped a 13-year-old girl and raped her. That person was here illegally and deported on numerous occasions and used falsified—all have used falsified documents.

To that end, Mr. Secretary, my question is: How will your Department screen these folks, including background checks, to ensure the security of the citizens of America? Especially when people that don't, you know, recognize or respect the law, terrorists, people with terrorist ties and affiliations or motives that won't use proper documentation and won't come forward, how can we as the American citizens be confident that this plan to screen up to 5 million people that came here knowingly unlawfully, in many cases—in many cases, not all, but many—how can we have any confidence, based on those examples that I have already cited, any confidence that your agency and that this policy is going to work?

Secretary JOHNSON. Based on the experience that we had with the program 2 years ago, I believe that we will be vigilant in terms of looking for fraud in the application process.

The other part of my answer to your question, sir, is, through our reprioritization, I want to get at the criminals. I want clearer guidance so that our ERO enforcement workforce has the ability and the capability and the resources and the time to go after the type of individuals that you cite.

Mr. PERRY. We want that, too, but, with all due respect, Mr. Chairman, I have no confidence and I don't think the American people have any confidence that that is going to work. We appreciate, you know, your hope. We appreciate that with the resources being targeting to those individuals, maybe it could be better. But I see no plan and you have given me no plan at this point with any specific metrics or anything like that.

We have been working on this for years. None of us want these people in our community. I have two daughters. Heaven forbid one of them falls prey to something like that, and I can come to you and say, "Well, what did you do about it?", and you said, "Well, we hoped for better." Mr. Secretary, that is just not an adequate answer.

Secretary JOHNSON. Well, that would not be——

Mr. PERRY. Thank you, Mr. Chairman. I yield back.

Secretary JOHNSON. That would not be an accurate characterization of my answer either.

I am happy to brief you and other Members of this committee on the implementation plan that CIS has put together. We have spent considerable time on it.

If you let me know the last time you sent me a letter that was unanswered and the date, I will be sure that it is answered.

Mr. PERRY. Thank you.

Chairman MCCAUL. Thank you, Mr. Secretary. Let me just say that I don't envy your position right now, but it has been a productive hearing. I think you have been forthright in your answers. It is a very emotional, divisive issue that I hope we can resolve in the Congress.

I can tell you this committee—and I think the Ranking Member feels the same way—we are committed to passing in the next Congress a border security bill, and we look forward to working with you on that.

Thanks for being here.

Secretary JOHNSON. Thank you.

Chairman MCCAUL. This hearing stands adjourned.

[Whereupon, at 11:16 a.m., the committee was adjourned.]

APPENDIX

QUESTIONS FROM HONORABLE SUSAN W. BROOKS FOR HONORABLE JEH C. JOHNSON

Question 1. In your testimony you said, "We encourage those undocumented immigrants who have been here for the last 5 years, have sons or daughters who are citizens or lawful permanent residents, and do not fall into one of our enforcement priorities to come out of the shadows, get on the books, and pass National security and criminal background checks." In this context, please explain what you mean exactly when you say to "get on the books"?

Answer. Response was not received at the time of publication.

Question 2. Under the current law and before the Executive Order, where did undocumented immigrants fit into the pipeline of those immigrants waiting to become citizens the legal way?

Now under the Executive Order, where do undocumented immigrants who are lawfully present fit into the pipeline of those currently waiting to become citizens the legal way?

Answer. Response was not received at the time of publication.

Question 3. From where is USCIS getting the funds to carry out this Executive Order?

Will resources be diverted away from those going through the legal process of becoming a citizen to carry out this Executive Order?

Answer. Response was not received at the time of publication.

www.ingramcontent.com/pod-product-compliance
Lightning Source LLC
Chambersburg PA
CBHW081114280526
45787CB00007B/2824